Oliver Twist

CHARLES DICKENS

Guide written by
Andrew Sprakes

A *Letts* EXPLORE **Literature Guide**

First published 1998

Letts Educational
Aldine House
Aldine Place
London W12 8AW
0181 740 2266

Text © Andrew Sprakes

Series editor Ron Simpson

Typeset by Jordan Publishing Design

Text design Jonathan Barnard

Cover and text illustrations Ivan Allen

Design © BPP (Letts Educational) Ltd

Acknowledgements
Outline answers are solely the responsibility of the author, and are not supplied or approved by the Exam Board.

British Library Cataloguing in Publication Data
A CIP record for this book is available from the British Library

ISBN 1 85758 865 7

Printed and bound in Great Britain

Ashford Colour Press, Gosport, Hampshire

Letts Educational is the trading name of BPP (Letts Educational) Ltd

Contents

Plot synopsis

The novel begins with the birth of Oliver and the death of his mother in child-birth. He is born a pauper and is raised in the harsh regime of the workhouse. Oliver spends his first nine years in a branch workhouse with other 'juveniles', and then is brought back to the main workhouse by the beadle, Mr Bumble. After suffering near starvation for three months the boys decide to draw lots to see who should ask for more food. The task falls to Oliver. His request is viewed as immoral and wicked by the workhouse board so he is removed from the care of the workhouse and is apprenticed to the undertaker, Mr Sowerberry, where his mistreatment continues. In desperation Oliver runs away and on the road to London meets up with Jack Dawkins (the artful Dodger) who takes Oliver to Fagin's den in Saffron Hill. Fagin is nurturing a gang of young thieves and receiving stolen goods from various criminals, such as the brutal and violent Bill Sikes, and Oliver is drawn innocently into a world of crime. Oliver is rescued from this underworld by Mr Brownlow only to be kidnapped by Sikes' companion, Nancy, to resume his life with Fagin and his gang.

Oliver's kidnap is due in part to Fagin's agreement with the character Monks, who is a mysterious villain with a keen interest in the destruction of Oliver. Oliver is sent on a dark mission with Sikes and his associates to burgle a house in the country. However, the crime goes horribly wrong, Oliver is shot by a servant and left for dead by Sikes. Oliver is saved by the owner of the house, Mrs Maylie, who takes pity on the innocent Oliver and together with her niece, Rose, determines to care for the stricken orphan.

Nancy eavesdrops on a conversation between Monks and Fagin in which they further plot the downfall and the destruction of Oliver and in which Monks suggests a connection between Rose Maylie and Oliver. Wanting to redeem herself in some way for kidnapping Oliver, whom she has become fond of, Nancy discloses what she knows to Rose Maylie and Mr Brownlow. The gang discovers that Nancy has revealed information which potentially puts them all at risk and she is savagely murdered by Sikes as reward for her seeming betrayal.

Mr Brownlow pursues his investigations and forces Monks to confess his true relationship to Oliver. Mr Brownlow reveals that Monks is indeed Oliver's half-brother, and his motive for Oliver's destruction is greed as he wishes to keep their father's inheritance to himself. A further disclosure confirms that Rose is Oliver's aunt, sister to his dead mother Agnes.

Fagin's gang is broken up and he is arrested and sentenced to death for his crimes. Sikes, whilst fleeing from an angry mob intent on bringing the murderer to justice, accidentally hangs himself from a rooftop. The novel ends with the condemnation of Fagin and the adoption of Oliver by Mr Brownlow.

Oliver

Oliver Twist

Oliver, the pauper's child and orphan, is the hero of the novel. The story begins with the birth of Oliver and we chart his progress throughout the course of the text. Oliver is shown to be kind-hearted and loving in the face of extreme suffering and hardship, and manages to maintain his innocence even when forced into an underworld of crime and violence. He is predominantly a victim of circumstance throughout the text and is mistreated and abused by various sections of society.

Oliver is seen by many readers as an idealised innocent, but his capacity to adapt to and survive at times brutal episodes in his life, presents Oliver as a much more complex and three-dimensional character than one would at first assume. Oliver's loving and determined nature is unaffected by environment and, in spite of all the difficulties he experiences, he remains upright and virtuous. The novel is mainly concerned with Oliver between the ages of nine and twelve. During that time Oliver matures from an innocent victim of the workhouse to a worthy young gentleman.

Fagin

Fagin

Perhaps one of the most notorious of all Dickens' creations is the classic villain, Fagin. From his introduction in Chapter 8 Fagin dominates the novel with his manipulative scheming and grovelling malice. He is a receiver of stolen goods and the leader of the pick-pocket gang that includes the artful Dodger. He is a colourful character and is strangely appealing in his wickedness. Indeed, the mock pick-pocketing scenes, when Oliver is first introduced to the den of thieves in Saffron Hill, provide the text with some lively humour. Compare the presentation of Fagin with that of Oliver. Which character is more convincing?

Although Fagin is shown to possess undesirable traits of selfishness, greed, cruelty and weakness he never ceases to engage the reader. Fagin is manipulative and has a hold over various characters in the novel, particularly Nancy who fears as well as hates him. Fagin inhabits a world of self interest, mistrust and disloyalty which finally leads to his destruction. His cruelty is best embodied by his willingness to work with Monks in bringing about the destruction of Oliver.

Fagin eventually pays the ultimate price for his crimes by losing his life. However, is it possible to feel sympathy for Fagin, in spite of all his previously immoral actions when, in the penultimate chapter, Dickens describes him as, 'cowered down upon his stone bed … His red hair hung down upon his bloodless face; his beard was torn, and twisted into knots; his eyes shone with a terrible light …'?

The artful Dodger

Jack Dawkins, 'the artful Dodger', is another memorable creation of Dickens'. He is the most accomplished pick-pocket employed by Fagin and it is he who first introduces Oliver to the gang of thieves at Saffron Hill. The Dodger is confident and self-assured and puts on the airs of a gentleman. His distinctive top hat is his trademark and even though he is a child his way of life has aged him prematurely. Although he does show Oliver some kindness the Dodger is committed to a life of crime and shows no remorse even at his trial towards the end of the novel.

Sikes and Nancy

Nancy, like the artful Dodger, is also a thief for Fagin. She was corrupted by Fagin as a child to steal for him and she fears and hates him. She knows she is doomed to a certain way of life and that she is trapped in a violent world of crime, and she accepts her fate with grim determination. She is by no means an innocent and, indeed, she is instrumental in kidnapping Oliver from Mr Brownlow and returning him to the terrifying clutches of Fagin. However, in spite of her environment and her conditioning, she shows that she has a sense of moral decency by attempting to help Oliver when she overhears the plans of Fagin and Monks. Her betrayal of the gang effectively brings about her murder by Sikes.

Sikes is Nancy's partner. He is a cruel, coarse and violent criminal. He abuses Nancy who clearly loves him, and to protect his own position he brutally murders her in one of the most shocking scenes ever written by Dickens. Sikes also mistreats Oliver and after the attempted burglary of the Maylie household leaves the wounded Oliver in a ditch without thought for whether he will live or die. In a novel with so many dark and evil characters Sikes is arguably the most frightening of all.

Mr Brownlow

Mr Brownlow takes Oliver into his care after the pick-pocketing incident. He is a generous and warm-hearted old gentleman who shows complete trust in Oliver. Behind Mr Brownlow's kindly nature lies a more complex personality. It is Mr Brownlow who Rose Maylie turns to for help and he masterminds the capture of Monks and forces his subsequent confession. His adoption of Oliver at the end of the text shows his enduring humanity.

Mr and Mrs Bumble

Whilst these two characters are the source of much humour in the novel it is difficult to feel any sympathy for them as the story concludes. Mr Bumble is shown throughout the text to be a bully and ultimately a coward. He is shown to be a very shallow character who is concerned only with his status and an overblown idea of his own importance. He enjoys having power over people less fortunate than himself and abuses that power.

Mrs Bumble is as bad if not worse than her husband. She is domineering and forceful and for her own gain is prepared to conspire with Monks to hide the identity of Oliver. In the end justice seems to be done as they both end up as paupers living in the workhouse themselves.

The workhouse and town characters

As well as Mr Bumble and Mrs Bumble, Dickens presents us with a number of other characters who inhabit the workhouse. Generally the characters who represent the workhouse board are unsympathetic, such as 'the gentleman in the white waistcoat', and they are used primarily for Dickens to make fun of (satirise) the system. Little Dick, Oliver's friend, is the only character who is remembered with fondness by Oliver from his time at the workhouse and, sadly, news of the weak child's death arrives towards the end of the novel. Indeed, to a certain extent, little Dick is hardly more than a symbol for poverty and suffering.

During Oliver's time at the workhouse we are also introduced to other characters who generally mistreat our hero. For instance, Mr Gamfield, the chimney sweep, is only interested in taking Oliver as an apprentice for the money he will receive from the workhouse for taking him. The Sowerberrys also victimise Oliver to such an extent that he eventually runs away.

The criminal underworld

Dickens fills the novel with interesting and engaging villains. The criminal underworld is crammed with mistrustful characters, from the renowned housebreaker Toby Crackit to the naive and stupid Tom Chitling. Most of the characters appear trapped, through either poverty or habit, in this life of crime. The two most striking exceptions are Noah Claypole, who appears to readily seek out the criminal element in London, and Charley Bates who, shocked and disgusted by Nancy's murder, succeeds, after many struggles, in leaving the life of crime behind him.

The Maylies

The characters who inhabit the world of the Maylies are in direct contrast to the criminal underworld in London. Mrs Maylie is kind and compassionate and does not hesitate in caring for Oliver when he arrives, seriously injured, on her doorstep after the bungled burglary. Rose Maylie, the adopted niece, is even more considerate, if this were possible! She is often described in angelic terms by Dickens, prompting some critics to believe she is almost too good to be true.

All of the characters connected with the Maylies, especially Mr Losberne, the doctor, and Harry Maylie, are all pleasant and worthy people, showing a sympathetic kindness towards Oliver and actively helping in restoring his birthright to him.

■ Themes in *Oliver Twist*

Crime

Crime

Crime is a central theme in *Oliver Twist*. Dickens presents a vivid picture of a nineteenth-century underworld through his presentation of Fagin and his gang. However, we are not meant merely to view crime but also to understand its effect on others. The criminal world inhabited by Fagin is, on the surface, lively and in some ways attractive, but underneath it is dangerous, violent and deadly.

As well as the organised crime of Fagin, Sikes and the Dodger, Dickens also presents us with the criminal activities of Monks, whose crime against Oliver is motivated purely by self-interest, greed and an inexplicable hatred.

The social and human cost of crime is obvious. Nancy, towards the end of the novel, is a pathetic figure because she cannot remove herself from the circle she is trapped in. She finally pays the ultimate price when misplaced loyalty to Sikes results in her murder by him. The world of crime in *Oliver Twist* is indeed a dark one and Dickens does not hesitate to present it in this way. Descriptions of place when associated with the criminal element are always gloomy, uninviting and depressing, where characters move around like threatening shadows.

As nineteenth-century readers would have expected, the criminals, for the most part, pay for their lives of crime: Fagin, Sikes and Nancy lose their lives, and the artful Dodger is transported. However, Dickens does allow some characters to find salvation: Charley Bates is an example that springs to mind. Other characters, it could be argued, even profit from crime, such as Noah Claypole, alias Morris Bolter who, at the end of the story, becomes an informer for the Bow Street Runners, the police force of that time. However, this would have been a dangerous occupation!

Whatever Dickens' moral outlook on crime, there is no doubt that the novel comes alive when he is writing about these characters. Fagin, like Dickens' other grotesque creations, such as Scrooge in *A Christmas Carol*, dominates the text and adds weight to the argument that Dickens seems to be at his best when writing about villains.

Poverty

Poverty

A direct cause of crime in the text is poverty. Many characters turn to a life of crime due to social problems. Nancy talks of being snared in Fagin's net out of need and desperation, and Dickens seems to suggest that for the poor the choice is either a life of misery and hardship in the workhouse or a life of crime. Poverty in the text seems to suggest a lack of choice and, for most characters, helplessness.

The novel begins in the workhouse with the paupers of the parish whose ranks Oliver is thrust into. Dickens shows the lives of the poor to be harsh and desperate. He attacks The Poor Law of 1834 (see note) and suggests that it increased the suffering of the poor rather than providing help. Indeed, conditions and treatment in the workhouse are appalling. The infamous gruel scene where Oliver asks for more suggests something of the dietary conditions. Most of the figures of authority who represent society in the novel, such as Mr Bumble the beadle, the gentleman in the white waistcoat on the workhouse board and Mr Fang the magistrate, treat the poor inhumanely and without sympathy. Even the poor who are not criminals are classed as such merely because they are poor.

The social and historical subject matter of the novel is therefore very important. Dickens purposely attacks the political and philosophical ideas of the time in a very sarcastic way – this is called **satire**. Dickens often pokes fun at society through his narration; he frequently writes one thing while clearly implying another – this is called **irony**. Sadly, the only way out of poverty in the text is to be rescued by kindly, compassionate people or to be lucky enough to be the long-lost relative of someone who is comfortably well off!

The Poor Law Amendment Act of 1834

The Poor Law provided relief for the poor by charging those who worked a Poor Law rate which was administered by local magistrates. In repayment the poor were occupied with menial jobs for the parish. This changed in 1834 – relief for the poor was now to be provided by placing them in workhouses. The Victorian attitude was that people were only poor because they were idle. The conditions in the workhouses were purposely uncomfortable and unappealing and led, at least in Dickens' opinion, to more hardship.

Loneliness

Loneliness

The theme of loneliness is predominantly shown through the central character of the text, Oliver. Right from the outset Oliver, through the death of his mother in child birth, is left alone. He remains isolated throughout much of the text except when he is briefly 'saved' by Mr Brownlow and, also, when he is looked after by the Maylies. Oliver's loneliness is only truly diminished when he finally comes to know of his true identity and background. As well as Oliver, many other characters experience loneliness and isolation in varying degrees. Rose Maylie believes that, due, like Oliver, to a dubious background, she will never marry or be truly accepted by society and this causes her much anguish. Nancy also experiences loneliness as her feelings for Sikes are, for the most part, unacknowledged by him. She seems to recognise a shadow of herself in Oliver and risks her life to help the young orphan. Her decision to do this isolates her from the criminal world she inhabits and, as she cannot leave Sikes, means that she dies for her actions.

Chance

Chance

Chance often drives the plot forward in *Oliver Twist* and adds exciting twists and turns to the narrative. Some critics feel that Dickens overuses chance and that it is, therefore, a weakness in the novel. However, the use of chance adds to the inevitability of the narrative as Fate closes in on the criminals at the centre of the crime and the intricate plotting adds to the mystery and suspense of the story. What is your opinion of the chance occurrences in the text? Do they add to the novel's effect or do you think Dickens relies too much on chance?

Essays/Examiner's tip icon

This icon is used to draw attention to a section of the **Text commentary** that is particularly relevant to either the section on **How to write a coursework essay** or to the section on **How to write an examination essay**. Each time it is used, a note identifies which section it relates to and adds a comment, quotation or piece of advice.

■ Text commentary

Oliver Twist was first issued in novel form in three volumes. However, most modern editions number the chapters through from 1 to 53, so this practice has been followed here. The self-test questions have been placed after significant points of action in the text.

Chapter 1

Oliver is born into the workhouse and, as he struggles for life, we witness the death of his mother who tragically dies after planting a first and final kiss upon her baby's forehead. The identity of the mother is unknown and remains a mystery, although it is clear the baby has been born out of wedlock and is, therefore, illegitimate. Oliver 'was badged and ticketed and fell into his place at once – a parish child – the orphan of the workhouse …'

The birth of Oliver

The first chapter is typical of Dickens' narrative style as he manages to make a number of satirical comments about the plight of the poor while introducing the main character. Oliver's unlucky origins set the tone of the novel and reflect the difficulties he is to face. There is heavy irony in the way that Dickens suggests that if Oliver had been surrounded by doting parents and fussing relatives he would have struggled for breath and died.

Oliver

However, Oliver finds himself in the uncaring environment of the workhouse and, because he is left alone, he manages to eventually gasp out a breath and so survives.

Many factors are stacked against the baby – the only people present at the birth are an indifferent parish surgeon and an old woman who has been drinking heavily. Indeed, Oliver is labelled immediately by the doctor, 'It's very likely it will be troublesome', and so his isolated life begins.

Loneliness

The chapter ends with the lines, 'Oliver cried lustily. If he could have known that he was an orphan, left to the tender mercies of churchwardens and overseers, perhaps he would have cried the louder.' Why do you think the chapter ends in this way? Does this suggest anything about Oliver's future?

Chapter 2

Oliver is sent, on the brink of starvation, to a branch workhouse run by Mrs Mann. Here other juvenile paupers are equally mistreated. Many of the children die of starvation; at other times they are thrashed for 'presuming to be hungry'. Mr Bumble, the beadle, visits the branch workhouse and shows the petty and bullying side of his nature. Mr Bumble has come on business: to take Oliver back to the workhouse proper as he has passed the age of nine. Oliver appears before the workhouse board and is set to work. The harsh regime of the workhouse causes suffering and hunger and, after drawing lots, it falls to Oliver to ask for more gruel. Oliver's request provokes outrage amongst the owners and is seen as a form of rebellion. Oliver is locked up and a reward of five pounds is offered to anyone who would take him 'off the hands of the parish.'

A further glimpse of Oliver

Oliver, at the age of nine, is described as, 'a pale thin child, somewhat diminutive in stature, and decidedly small in circumference. But nature or inheritance had implanted a good sturdy spirit in Oliver's breast.' Contrast here the physical description with the spiritual: Oliver has an inner strength, which is to enable his survival throughout the text.

Oliver

The introduction of the beadle

It is worth noting that Mr Bumble's first action in the novel is a violent one

as he kicks the gate which has been bolted by Mrs Mann so that Oliver and the other orphans can be spruced up. He is described unfavourably by Dickens from the outset, 'Mr Bumble was a fat man, and a choleric one …', which shows that he is not only well-fed in comparison to Oliver, but also that he is bad tempered and given to outbursts of anger.

Mr and Mrs Bumble

Dickens goes on to show that he is pompous and full of a sense of his own importance, 'Mr Bumble had a great idea of his oratorical powers and his importance.' He is vain and enjoys the power his office brings; he 'glanced complacently at the cocked hat and smiled. Yes, he smiled. Beadles are but men; and Mr Bumble smiled.' What does Mr Bumble's name suggest about his character? Are names important in influencing your views on any other characters in the novel? Compare the introduction of Mr Bumble with his last appearance in the novel in Chapter 51. How much does Bumble change over the course of the novel? Do you think he learns anything from his experiences?

Oliver in front of the workhouse board

In this section notice the contrast between Oliver on one hand and Mr Bumble and the board on the other. The fat, well-fed, round-faced board

Poverty

members treat Oliver without any sensitivity or care. Look at the presentation of 'the gentleman in the white waistcoat' who constantly bullies and insults Oliver. At this point Dickens attacks the Poor Law and the thinking behind it, 'they established the rule, that all poor people should have the alternative… of being starved by gradual process in the house, or by a quick one out of it.' The workhouse, instead of providing protection for the poor becomes, in Dickens' opinion, a place where people starve and families are split up; it becomes a means to solve the problem of poverty by bringing about the death of the poor.

Chapter 3

Oliver is mistreated further when he is physically beaten in front of the other boys and imprisoned for his crime of asking for more food. Mr Gamfield, the chimney sweep, sees the reward of five pounds for taking Oliver away from the workhouse as an apprentice and makes a deal with Mr Bumble and the workhouse board. However, before the magistrate signs Oliver over to the chimney sweep he notices the fear on the young orphan's face. He allows Oliver to speak and the boy begs the magistrate not to send him away with the dreadful chimney sweep. Showing kindness the magistrate refuses to sign the papers and Oliver is saved from a terrible fate.

Social issues and poverty

Compare Oliver's treatment at the beginning of this chapter with Billy Casper's at school in *A Kestrel for a Knave*. Both receive corporal punishment (caning). Are the two boys bullied in a similar way? Do any characters show kindness? See the question on page 54.

Mr Gamfield, the chimney sweep

Gamfield is used as another example of how the poor were abused in these

Poverty

times. He is a cruel man, as we see from his treatment of his donkey, and he is keen to have Oliver for all the wrong reasons: mainly because he needs the money which is offered for taking Oliver on, and because Oliver will not eat much as he is used to a workhouse diet. The job of chimney sweep's boy was extremely dangerous and many children were killed as a result of climbing down chimneys. The risks of getting stuck, suffocating and being burned were just some of the hazards; as Dickens states, Mr Gamfield has 'bruised three or four boys to death already.'

Chapter 4

Following a discussion between Mr Bumble and Mr Sowerberry the undertaker, Oliver begins a new career working as an apprentice to Sowerberry. Oliver is led to his new home by Mr Bumble and is left at the mercy of Mrs Sowerberry. Note again Dickens' attack on the Workhouse 'gentlemen'. They, it appears, are quite prepared to ship Oliver out to a fate of violent abuse without consideration for his care or safety.

Mr Bumble jokes about death

Mr Bumble's character is revealed as he jokes about the number of infant deaths. When Sowerberry moans that the price for burying the poor from the workhouse is 'very small'. Bumble replies, 'So are the coffins'. What is your reaction to Mr Bumble? Does Dickens intentionally make him disgusting? All of Bumble's authority is in his outward trappings – his 'official coat' with its 'gilt-edged lappel'. Sowerberry exclaims 'You know – dear me, what a very elegant button this is, Mr Bumble.' But Bumble loses his temper when his credibility is called into question by Sowerberry, again demonstrating his pride and vanity.

Loneliness

Oliver is led away to a 'new scene of suffering' and he begins to cry. Do we accept this show of emotion from Oliver, or is Dickens being over-sentimental with his main character? We see Oliver's loneliness as Mrs Sowerberry criticises his tears and pushes him down the stairs into the coal cellar. Oliver is given the dog's leftovers and his hunger is made vividly clear by Dickens: 'I wish some well-fed philosopher... could have witnessed the horrible avidity with which Oliver tore bits asunder with all the ferocity of famine'. Oliver is led away to sleep by the coffins.

Chapter 5

The environment of the undertaker's parlour scares Oliver (who is now ten years old) and increases his feelings of loneliness and desolation. Oliver is bullied by Noah Claypole, a charity-boy (see below) who also works for Sowerberry. After a month Oliver is given the job of 'mute', walking in front of the coffin during a funeral procession. Oliver witnesses a funeral which is rushed (four minutes) as the people are poor. We see Oliver's loneliness once more: 'The boy had no friends to care for or to care for him'.

We meet Noah Claypole

Claypole's first action is to threaten Oliver. He comes from a Charity School; these school provided a less-than-basic education for the very poor. Claypole is thus referred to as a 'charity-boy' by Dickens, who shows the hypocrisy of Claypole – he has been bullied by local boys calling him 'charity' and 'leathers' (part of the Charity School's uniform was leather trousers), but he bullies

Oliver. He abuses Oliver Because Oliver is socially beneath him. The poverty of Oliver's environment is brought home to the reader by the fact that even the rats are hungry and are 'hideous with famine'.

Poverty

Compare the relationship between Mr and Mrs Sowerberry and that, later on, of Mr and Mrs Bumble. What similarities are there?

Chapter 6

Oliver settles into his profession. His mistreatment by Noah Claypole continues until Oliver is pushed too far and attacks Noah, who has insulted his mother. Noah is saved by Charlotte, the Sowerberrys' daughter, and Mrs Sowerberry who 'pummel' Oliver and lock him in the dust cellar. Mr Bumble is sent for.

Childhood

Oliver does show that when he is roused he will stand up for himself: 'Crimson with fury, Oliver started up, overthrew the chair and the table.'

Oliver fights back

Oliver shows that when he is roused he has the capacity to act and react. When

Noah taunts Oliver and eventually insults his dead mother, Oliver becomes 'Crimson with fury'. As soon as Oliver attacks him Noah shows his true colours; his cowardice is shown perfectly by Dickens as the boy, after Oliver has hurt him, begins to 'blubber' like a baby.

Oliver

Do we see a different side to Oliver here? Does it make him a more convincing character?

Environment

Is this an example of how environment can cause individuals to react in a certain way? Would you have expected Oliver to behave in this manner? What are the factors that bring about his rage?

Chapter 7

Noah relates Oliver's sins to Mr Bumble. Oliver is still enraged and even dares to show no fear of Mr Bumble. Oliver continues to rebel when released and stands up to Mrs Sowerberry. He is beaten by Sowerberry and ordered upstairs for the night. In the

morning Oliver runs away. He passes the workhouse and sees Dick, a friend and playmate. Oliver bids him goodbye.

Oliver runs away

Oliver

Oliver's boldness is apparent in this chapter and he even manages to stagger Mr Bumble. He displays 'bravery' in the face of abuse, and it is only when on his own that he allows himself to cry. Oliver's reason for running away is the cruelty he has faced. It is significant that his mistreatment leaves him with no apparent option but to take his chances in the outside world.

A sentimental character

Little Dick is presented sentimentally by Dickens. He is weak and feeble and seems powerless to act. He appears to be resigned to his lot and sadly bids Oliver farewell. Why do you think Dickens includes a character like Dick at this point? Is he trying to say something about the poor in general and highlight their terrible oppression? Or is Dick meant to be a reminder to the reader that Oliver is not going to passively accept his lifestyle, but will actively try to change it?

Chapter 8

Oliver decides to run away to London so that he cannot be found. He walks twenty miles in a day and sleeps in a field. The next day he covers twelve miles. He meets with mistrust and some cruelty along the way, although two people show him kindness. He arrives at Barnet after six days of travel and is lonely, desolate and suffering. Oliver meets Jack Dawkins (the artful Dodger), who buys him some food and drink and offers him shelter. They arrive in London at Saffron Hill. After a password is given they are admitted to Fagin's den. Oliver meets Fagin and his gang, eats supper then falls asleep. Oliver's naivety and innocence are evident as he seems to have little or no idea that London can pose a threat or be dangerous.

Introduction of the artful Dodger

The artful Dodger

Crime

Dickens paints a vivid and colourful description of the Dodger, and shows the complexity of his character. He is a boy but has the mannerisms of a man. He is at once appealing, yet dirty. We are as dazzled by the appearance and language of the Dodger as Oliver is supposed to be.

Dickens hints that the Dodger is associated with crime by the language that he uses. For example, 'beak' for magistrate and 'mill' for jail. The Dodger already has an hidden agenda for Oliver; look at the way he 'eyed him' and gave him 'close observation', as if he is examining a product that can be used. It is clear that the Dodger has determined Oliver's innocence by stating to Charley that he found Oliver in 'Greenland', 'green' of course being a word associated with naivety.

Fagin welcomes his new guest

Fagin

Look at the description of Fagin: he is 'repulsive', with matted 'red hair', almost suggesting he is the devil incarnate. Examine other descriptions of Fagin throughout the rest of the novel. Does Dickens succeed in creating a monster?

Examiner's tip

Look carefully at the way the artful Dodger and Fagin are introduced to the text. What is interesting about their presentation? How do their personalities compare with that of little Dick, for instance? See the question on page 57.

Crime

Children are made into adults in this environment, and there is a loss of innocence. Oliver is frisked without even realising it, which again shows his innocence. Fagin acts as a mock gentleman and attempts to convey a show of respectability. In fact, many of the scenes in Fagin's den are almost theatrical. Why might this be and what effect does it create? It is clear, however, that Oliver has been led into a crime-ridden environment, which is confirmed with the obvious evidence of stolen goods in the form of pocket handkerchiefs.

Chapter 9

Oliver slowly wakes up and in his drowsiness sees Fagin at his hiding place for his valuables. Fagin reacts violently when he notices that Oliver has seen him, but when he realises how innocent Oliver is he calms down. The Dodger and Charley Bates, one of Fagin's crew, return from a pick-pocketing spree and show their spoils. The Dodger and Charley show Oliver how to pick-pocket in an elaborate 'game' with Fagin as the 'victim'. The boys leave, rewarded for their work, with Nancy and Bet. Fagin attempts to teach Oliver the 'art' of pick-pocketing, showing him how to unpick the initials on the stolen handkerchiefs.

The presentation of Charley

Crime

Charley is a positive character who brings humour to the scenarios he is in. He focuses on Oliver's innocence and calls him 'green'. The echoes of Charley's laughter can be heard at intervals throughout the rest of the text. At the end of the novel, because Charley has been presented as a frivolous and light-hearted character, his disgust of Sikes has added impact.

Here, the subculture of crime is shown clearly to the reader by Dickens,

Crime

yet Oliver remains totally innocent! Oliver sees the pick-pocketing and robbing of Fagin as a 'game', as Nancy and Bet join in. We see Fagin's greed and miserliness in this chapter as he hoards the stolen goods of criminals who have suffered capital punishment – a reminder of the possible rewards of a life of crime. On the other hand we see the material spoils of the Dodger's and Charley's work.

Chapter 10

Oliver joins the Dodger and Charley on a thieving spree. Oliver discovers that their 'work' is indeed stealing as they take a handkerchief from a man absorbed in reading a book. Oliver is both horrified and amazed; he runs from the crime scene and, despite his innocence, is wrongly accused of the theft when he is captured.

An innocent is shocked

The petty thieving of Charley 'by pilfering diverse apples and onions…',

Crime

results in Oliver wanting to 'seek his way back' as he does not want to be involved in these illegal activities. Oliver is clearly shocked and stunned by the boys' behaviour and watches in 'silent amazement'. It is worth considering the Dodger's and Charley's behaviour: they contribute to 'the hue and cry' and pursue Oliver to deflect any suspicion from themselves. Note

that when describing the pursuit Dickens writes in the present tense. What effect does this have? Does it make the chase more exciting? Why do you think so much speech is used at this point by many unknown characters?

Social issues and poverty

Oliver tries to disassociate himself from the criminal actions of the Dodger and Charley in the same way that Billy Casper, in *A Kestrel for a Knave*, tries to break away from McDowall's gang. Both characters realise crime is wrong, yet Billy still steals but Oliver will not. Why is this? See the question on page 54.

Chapter 11

Oliver is taken by the police officer to go before the infamous magistrate Mr Fang, known for his severity. Oliver, overcome by Mr Fang's cruel bullying and the situation, faints. He is sentenced to three months 'hard labour' until he is saved by the testimony of the bookstall owner who saw the whole incident. The case is dismissed and Oliver, clearly distressed and in ill health, is taken into Mr Brownlow's care.

The gentleman and Mr Fang

Mr Fang, the magistrate, is a frightening figure and offers no sympathy to

Oliver. The contrasting persona of Mr Brownlow is interesting here, as he speaks to Mr Fang 'like a gentleman', though he clearly does not behave like one. Mr Brownlow is compassionate and obviously concerned about Oliver's health. The court proceedings are ridiculous; Mr Fang is a bully and believes Oliver is pretending to be ill to get off with the charge. There is little evidence against Oliver, and Mr Brownlow, the gentleman who has been robbed, does not wish to press charges. Mr Fang even tries to suggest that Mr Brownlow simply wants to cover up his own theft of a book which he has inadvertently held onto whilst chasing the suspected criminal, Oliver.

Mr Brownlow

Look at the words associated with Mr Brownlow up to this point. He has

shown nothing but concern and compassion for Oliver and yet, after the provocation of Mr Fang, he is in a 'frenzy of rage and defiance'. The irony here is that, rather than the crime which has been committed against Mr Brownlow upsetting him, it is the workings of criminal law that have got him into a frenzy.

Chapter 12

Oliver wakes up in Mr Brownlow's house, and is treated with kindness and compassion by Mrs Bedwin, the housekeeper. After Oliver has recovered from the fever, Mr Brownlow comes to talk to him. The chapter includes the revelation that a portrait hanging on Mr Brownlow's wall bears a startling resemblance to Oliver. At the end of the chapter the spotlight returns to the Dodger and Charley Bates who return to Fagin's hideout without Oliver.

The importance of a portrait

In this chapter a portrait is mentioned which is described as 'A living copy' of Oliver. What is the importance of the portrait? Oliver's mother is also mentioned here. Why does Dickens do this at this point? Is it to create a sentimental picture of Oliver or is it for plot reasons? What do you find out later on about Oliver's mother?

Oliver

Chapter 13

Fagin reacts violently to the news of Oliver's capture and he assaults Charley and the Dodger by hurling a pot at them, nearly striking Bill Sikes, who has just entered. They decide to find out from the magistrate what has happened to Oliver, in order to kidnap him back and ensure his silence. Nancy is sent to the court and discovers that Oliver has been taken by a gentleman. Sikes leaves the den quickly, and Oliver's life is in danger, as Fagin threatens to 'stop his mouth'.

An engaging ruffian

Sikes and Nancy

The description of Bill Sikes is dramatic. He is clearly a violent and coarse man. Look at the way he treats his dog, Bulls-eye, for example. His speech is crude and he is openly threatening to Fagin. Why do you think Dickens uses 'growled a deep voice' to describe the first thing said by Sikes? What impression does this give you of Sikes? What kind of temperament do you think he has?

Crime

Sikes calls Fagin a 'fence', meaning someone who receives stolen goods and sells them on. The relationship between characters is shown here. Fagin ill-treats the boys, but Sikes is aggressive towards Fagin. All the characters show mistrust and even hatred towards each other. The relationship between Sikes and Nancy demonstrates this as Sikes threateningly says, 'she will go' when Nancy initially refuses to visit the police cells in search of Oliver. Nancy shows that she can put on an act at the magistrates too. She is by no means an innocent.

■ Self-test questions Chapters 1–13

Who? What? Why? When? Where? How?
1 Who does Oliver meet in Barnet?
2 What does Mr Gamfield do for a living?
3 Why does Nancy visit the cells at the police office?
4 When does Oliver run away?
5 Where does Mr Brownlow live?
6 How far does Oliver walk on the first day of his journey to London?
7 Who gives Oliver his name?
8 What passwords does the artful Dodger use to gain entrance to Fagin's den?
9 Why does Oliver attack Noah Claypole?
10 When does Oliver ask for more gruel?
11 Where does Oliver see Little Dick?
12 How much money does Mr Sowerberry receive for taking Oliver as an apprentice?

Who said this about whom?
1 'What's the charge against this boy? What have you got to say, sir?'
2 'Why, you're quite a literary character, sir!'
3 'I never was more convinced of anything in my life, than I am that that boy will come to be hung.'
4 'What a grateful little dear it is. Pretty creetur!'
5 'You're a rough speaker, my friend, but you look an honest, open-hearted man.'

Open quotations

Complete the following quotations.

1 'Dead men never repent; ...'
2 ' "Please, sir," replied Oliver, ...'
3 'If he means to blab us among his new friends ...'
4 'You're an insolent impertinent fellow ...'

Prove it!

1 What is Dickens' view of the workhouses? Give examples to support your answer.
2 What evidence is there that Oliver will never turn to a life of crime?
3 'the law is a ass; a idiot.' Mr Bumble makes this comment towards the end of the novel, but is this a fair reflection of the legal system in this section?

Chapter 14

Oliver continues his recuperation at Mr Brownlow's, and is treated well. Mr Brownlow interviews Oliver in his book-filled study and, although Oliver fears being sent away, he is asked to tell his life story. This is interrupted by a visit from Mr Grimwig, a friend of Brownlow's, who believes that Oliver will try to steal from the house. To show his complete faith in Oliver, Brownlow sends him to return some books and pay a bill. Grimwig states that Oliver will not return. Oliver is pleased to be of service to Mr Brownlow and runs the errand. The two gentlemen wait expectantly for his return.

Kindness at last

Compare the treatment of Oliver by Mrs Bedwin with his treatment by Bumble, Sowerberry and Fagin. This is the first time in his life, and Oliver is ten at this point, that he has been treated with any consistent kindness. Oliver is tidied up and is even allowed to sell his old clothes. It is almost as if Oliver's clothes represent his dreadful past and he is glad to be rid of them. Clothes are often seen as a status symbol in the text. Can you identify any other times when clothes are used in this way?

Oliver

Social issues and poverty

Oliver does receive some kindness in a home environment, although for much of the text he is denied this. Compare Oliver's different homes in the workhouse, at Mr Brownlow's, in Fagin's den and at the Maylies' with Billy Casper's home life in *A Kestrel for a Knave*. What are the similarities? What are the differences? See the question on page 54.

The introduction of Mr Grimwig

Mr Grimwig is an eccentric character; in keeping with his slightly absurd character he rambles on about the orange peel on the stairs having tripped him up. He is described as 'irascible' (meaning ill-tempered), 'growling' and 'fierce'. He seems to enjoy contradicting Mr Brownlow even though the two are friends. Grimwig is used almost to counteract Brownlow's faith in Oliver. Look at the wager between the two gentlemen in this chapter. Is Brownlow to blame for sending Oliver out or is it Grimwig? Dickens suggests that Grimwig is not a 'bad-hearted' man and he goes on to prove this towards the end of the novel.

Chapter 15

The criminal gang is still keen to get back Oliver, who takes a wrong turn on his way to the bookseller and is grabbed by Nancy. She pretends Oliver is her lost brother. Sikes arrives and beats Oliver. Meanwhile, Mrs Bedwin, Brownlow and Grimwig wait anxiously for Oliver's return. Oliver is taken back to Fagin's den and the journey is described almost as if it is a descent into hell.

Sikes' relationship with Fagin

Consider the way Dickens creates a vivid picture of Sikes. The chapter starts with a gloomy description of Sikes and his dog in the drab parlour of a public house in a filthy part of town. Look at the language Dickens uses when describing the brooding man and his unpleasant dog. There is more evidence of Sikes' violent nature as he fights with his dog, again, and later beats Oliver.

We see once more how closely linked the characters are when Sikes says to Fagin 'If I go you go'. The mistrust and hatred between Sikes and Fagin is evident, and we are told that after Sikes' departure Fagin looked after him and 'shook his clenched fist; muttered a deep curse'. The events in this chapter are framed by characters, particularly Sikes and Fagin, not wishing to give anything away.

Chapter 16

Oliver is taken back to Fagin's den. When he tries to escape, Nancy stops the others beating him. Oliver realises Mr Brownlow will think he has stolen the books. His new clothes are removed.

The relationship between Sikes and Nancy

Nancy is scared that Sikes will end up being hanged, and tries to show him warmth but he is cold and hard. Why is it significant that Oliver notices that 'her hand trembles' and that her face turns 'deadly white'? Nancy shows a glimpse of humanity; as Oliver tries to escape she asks Sikes to call off the dog. She stands up for Oliver again when Fagin begins to beat him with a club, but she fights violence with violence. What is your view of Nancy at this point? She has been a key element in Oliver's capture, but now stands up for him. What does this show about her character? Nancy realises what she has done in bringing Oliver back – she has spoiled the good life he would have had with Mr Brownlow.

Environment

Nancy feels that Oliver will be changed by his environment, 'He's a thief, a liar, a devil, all that's bad from this night forth.'

It is made apparent that Nancy was taken into Fagin's 'care' at an early age and forced into a life of crime. It must be assumed that Nancy was an orphan, like Oliver, and that her poverty has led to her way of life.

Poverty

Chapter 17

Mr Bumble visits Mrs Mann and during their conversation we learn he is to travel to London on workhouse business. While there, Bumble sees an advertisement for the reward for Oliver Twist. Bumble contacts Brownlow and paints a picture of Oliver as an ungrateful and treacherous scoundrel. Subsequently, Mr Brownlow says that he never wants to hear Oliver's name again.

A very important man

As Dickens himself states at the opening of the chapter, we move from the

tragic to the comic. Mr Bumble is again shown as absurdly proud and full of his own importance. Once more Dickens focuses on Bumble's clothes as he walks through the streets. Mrs Mann's hypocrisy is noteworthy here too. She curses the fact that the beadle is visiting her as she is not ready for him, yet once Mr Bumble enters the workhouse Mrs Mann flatters and praises him.

Little Dick is the epitome of mistreatment. Bumble makes a ludicrous false evaluation of the child's character as he accuses Dick of being bad-tempered and vicious! Little Dick's request that before he dies he would like someone to write a note to

Poverty

Oliver, sending him his love, is met with cruelty by Mr Bumble and Mrs Mann.

Note the contrasting views of Oliver in this chapter – Bumble delivers a character assassination of him to Mr Brownlow, while Mrs Bedwin, at the end of the chapter, shows that she still believes in Oliver and refuses to accept that he has run away on purpose.

Five guineas reward

Chance

Chance plays a key part in Oliver's destiny. Mr Bumble sees the advertisement, which has been placed in the paper by Mr Brownlow, requesting information about Oliver Twist. Seeing the opportunity to make some easy money the beadle visits Mr Brownlow and gives him a prejudiced view of Oliver as a scoundrel. Mr Brownlow is deeply saddened by the information but is prepared to accept the beadle's word. Does this make Brownlow's character more believable?

Chapter 18

Oliver is held a virtual prisoner by Fagin. The Dodger tries to convince Oliver to accept Fagin's ways and become a thief, which Oliver does not want to do, but after so long locked up he is keen for any company so listens to what Dodger and Charley have to say. Fagin attempts to corrupt his character.

Fagin's plan

Fagin

Fagin terrifies Oliver with stories of hanging and suggests that if he does not do as he is told this is the fate which awaits him. Fagin then isolates Oliver and keeps him as a virtual prisoner for over a week. Oliver is so desperate for company that when he is released he is glad to sit with the Dodger and Charley. They try and convince Oliver that he should work for Fagin in order to make his life more bearable. Oliver is accepted back into the company of thieves and even enjoys some of the stories that Fagin tells of past robberies. Oliver resists to a certain extent, but Fagin hopes that he is beginning to break the young innocent. The sinister side of Fagin's character is evident in this chapter. Notice how many times Fagin enters 'unseen'. What effect does this have on our view of Fagin's character?

Environment

Fagin attempts to deny Oliver company to such an extent that he will enjoy any company at all. Oliver is accordingly affected by his environment, 'Oliver could not help laughing heartily, and showing that he was amused in spite of his better feelings.'

There are two aspects of the criminals' lives presented here. Look at the way in which 'hanging' is mentioned in such a nonchalant way in this chapter. The characters accept capital punishment as an occupational hazard; hanging

Crime

was indeed a part of life. In addition, it is worth noticing again the use of criminal slang: 'scragging' for hanging, 'fogles' for handkerchiefs and 'tickers' for watches. Does this add to the lively and interesting presentation of the criminal element?

Chapter 19

Fagin visits Bill Sikes and they discuss a burglary at a house in Chertsey. Sikes needs a small boy to climb through a window into a house, and Fagin suggests that Oliver would be perfect. We have a foreboding description of Oliver the night before he is handed over to Sikes for the burglary.

A loathsome reptile

Fagin

The description of Fagin at the opening of Chapter 19 is, indeed, a memorable one. As Fagin walks through the dark and poverty-stricken streets he appears to glide like a phantom. The weather, too, seems to reflect the dark and dismal character of Fagin. Fagin is keen to get Oliver involved in a crime so that his hold over Oliver will strengthen.

Another side to Nancy?

Sikes and Nancy

There is a code amongst criminals not to pass on information about each other, and Sikes says of Nancy, 'she ain't one to blab. Are you Nancy?'. Look at Nancy's reaction: she would never inform. How are we to view Nancy at this point? It appears that she is resigned to the fact that Fagin wishes to use Oliver in the robbery, and to a certain extent she encourages Sikes to take him. Why do you think she does this?

Chapter 20

Fagin warns Oliver about Sikes. Nancy arrives to take Oliver to Sikes and, although she shows some kindness, warns him not to cry out in the streets. When they arrive at Sikes' house, he shows Oliver a pistol, saying he will shoot him if he doesn't do exactly as he says. Sikes leads Oliver away.

Fagin's warning

Fagin appears to take some ghastly delight in the fact that Oliver is to be used

Crime

on the robbery. He scares Oliver and warns him about Bill Sikes' temper. Once again Oliver's innocence is shown as he has no idea of the plans that have been made for him. Fagin gives Oliver a book to read about the 'history of the lives and

trials of great criminals', which tells of terrible, blood-thirsty crimes. Oliver is so frightened he prays for protection and at that moment Nancy appears.

Does Dickens hint that Nancy is to be Oliver's salvation? Nancy is seen as a tragic figure and a victim; she shows Oliver that she has been physically abused by the brutal Sikes and that he must do exactly as Sikes directs or he will suffer the same fate.

A short lesson

Nancy's warning of Sikes' capacity for violence is confirmed by the man himself when Nancy and Oliver finally arrive at the robber's house. Sikes threatens Oliver with a pistol and suggests that, if necessary, he will use it. Sikes even puts the loaded gun to Oliver's head and warns that if he speaks out of turn he will shoot him.

Sikes plays on the knowledge that Oliver is alone in the world by suggesting that if he did have to kill Oliver no one would be bothered and no one would notice that he had gone missing. There is a chilling truth in what Sikes says.

Loneliness

Chapter 21

Sikes and Oliver journey through London and into the country. Oliver is scared and bewildered. They eventually arrive at a derelict house. Oliver's loneliness reaches new heights.

A cheerless morning

Oliver is led by Sikes on a whirlwind journey through the early morning streets of London. The hustle and bustle of the capital's streets add to Oliver's bewilderment. Dickens' narrative style adds to the effect as he packs the chapter with details of different places and people. Once they reach the countryside Oliver suddenly thinks that Sikes is going to murder him as they stop at a riverbank. It is here the rest of the gang is waiting in a derelict house.

Chapter 22

The house is a hideout used by the housebreakers. Toby Crackit and Barney are waiting for Bill and Oliver. At half past one they leave the house to commit the crime. As they approach the house, Oliver realises what they are about to do and panics. He is threatened and forced to enter the house through a small lattice window. Once in the house, Oliver is discovered and shot. Sikes pulls Oliver back through the window just before he passes out.

A description of Mr Crackit

Crime

We are now introduced to another larger-than-life character. Look at Dickens' description of Toby Crackit's clothes. Again, he presents a criminal who is a mixture of garish colour and filthy drabness. Is Crackit appealing, repulsive, or a combination of both?

A dreadful realisation

Oliver only realises what is going to take place as the criminals approach the

Oliver

house to be burgled. Oliver is so virtuous that he physically collapses at the thought of wrongdoing. Whatever your view of Oliver, it is interesting that he is prepared to risk his life at this point. Dickens has to maintain the moral integrity of his central character. Even though he is forced at gun point to climb through the window Oliver has every intention of

alerting the people of the house to the burglary. Dickens leaves us with a cliff-hanging ending to the chapter as, just before he can raise the alarm, Oliver is shot by residents of the house and is hauled through the window by Sikes.

Chapter 23

Mr Bumble visits Mrs Corney, a widow and matron of the workhouse. Bumble kisses her, but their love-making is disturbed by the news that Old Sally is dying and has something important to tell Mrs Corney.

A bitter world

Dickens opens the chapter with a harrowing description of the homeless and

Poverty

their struggle to stay alive against the bitterly cold weather. Contrast their plight with the comfort of Mrs Corney. She is unconcerned about the plight of the poor and yet it is her job to look after them.

Mr and Mrs Bumble

In this chapter Mr Bumble once again shows his harshness and insensitivity towards the poor. There is a dark humour to Mr Bumble's stories of blatant mistreatment of the hungry and dispossessed. Look at the clumsy compliments of Bumble's love-making, and the contrast of emotion when Mrs Corney is told that Old Sally is about to die. While she is out of the room Bumble greedily calculates her material wealth and decides that Mrs Corney is worth marrying!

Chapter 24

Mrs Corney hears Sally confess, on her death bed, that she stole something from a dying woman many years ago.

A confession

This is a key chapter as it gives us an important clue to Oliver's identity. As Old Sally dies she confesses to Mrs Corney that she once stole a locket and a ring from a young woman who died in the workhouse. Why do you think Dickens includes the two old crones, Anny and Martha, in this chapter? What is their importance later on in the text? Do you believe Mrs Corney's final comment that Old Sally had nothing of importance to say?

Chapter 25

Fagin and his gang are playing whist when Toby Crackit arrives and says that the burglary has gone terribly wrong. Oliver has been left for dead in a ditch.

Some disturbing news

The game of cards at Fagin's is disturbed by the return of Toby Crackit with

Crime
news of the failed burglary. The first person Toby asks after is Sikes as the two had been separated in their escape. Fagin obviously has had no contact with Sikes as he turns pale with fear at the question. Look at Fagin's reaction to Toby's return and the news he brings. Why does he react in this way?

Chapter 26

Fagin visits Saffron Hill and the Three Cripples Inn to get news of Sikes and also to enquire about a mysterious character named Monks. He arranges with the landlord to meet Monks later that night. Fagin goes to Sikes' house and, in a desperate rage, discloses to Nancy that Oliver is worth 'hundreds of pounds'. He must get Oliver back. Nancy is drunk so he is not too concerned about his outburst. On his return home he is met on the street by Monks. In a room on the first floor of Fagin's den they talk about Oliver, and Monks betrays the fact that he wishes to get rid of him. Monks sees the shadow of a woman pass by the window and believes that the conversation has been overheard, but when they investigate, no one is in sight.

Examiners' tip

Dickens vividly describes the crime-ridden environment inhabited by Fagin as he walks to the Three Cripples Inn. It is worth reading this chapter carefully as Dickens presents us with the physical and social effects of crime. See the question on page 57.

A visit to The Three Cripples

Fagin's search for Sikes at the 'Cripples' is fruitless. He eventually arrives at Sikes' residence and finds Nancy a little worse for drink. She has heard no news of Sikes either. It is significant that Fagin loses control a little here and

reveals that it is the loss of Oliver which is disturbing him, not the disappearance of Sikes. Nancy's reaction is also worth noting: she is pleased that Oliver is out of Fagin's grasp and out of her sight. She admits that Oliver seems to bring out her better feelings. She even hints that she could betray herself and all of Fagin's gang for the innocent orphan.

A dark figure

It is interesting to note the way in which Dickens presents Monks. He is shrouded in mystery, often referred to as a 'devil', and suddenly appears like some kind of spectre. When he moves, he 'glides', which adds to his ghostly presence.

A secret meeting

The meeting between Monks and Fagin is an extremely secretive one and

Fagin's treachery is shown through his admission that he has attempted to corrupt and destroy Oliver on Monks' behalf. It is revealed that Monks had seen Oliver when he was arrested for pick-pocketing, and that there is some reason for his hatred of the boy. If Oliver is found Fagin resolves to turn him to a life of crime. What makes this a particularly

disturbing chapter?

> ### Environment
> Oliver is shown to have an exceptional character and an inner strength: in spite of the environment he has found himself in, he is incorruptible. ' "I saw it was not easy to train him to the business," replied the Jew; "he was not like other boys in the same circumstances." '

Chapter 27

We return to Mr Bumble who, after checking Mrs Corney's possessions, asks for her hand in marriage and after she returns from Old Sally's deathbed she agrees. Bumble visits Sowerberry for a coffin for Old Sally and, looking through the parlour window, sees Noah Claypole being fed oysters by Charlotte Sowerberry. Just before Charlotte kisses Noah, Bumble bursts in and stops their improper behaviour.

'Mr Bumble had re-counted the teaspoons ...'

The shallowness of Mr Bumble's character is shown clearly by Dickens in this chapter. It is made apparent that one of the main reasons Bumble decides to marry Mrs Corney is based on possessions. Their hypocrisy is also highlighted when they suggest that they are only having a drink because it is medicinal and brings comfort.

Mr Bumble believes he will become workhouse master

Dickens presents us with the contrast between the poor and the better off.

Poverty

Mr Bumble moves from the pauper's ward in the workhouse, where he abuses the men as he passes, to the funeral parlour where Noah Claypole is being fed oysters by Charlotte. There is irony in this episode as Mr Bumble has just been enjoying a drink and then he condemns Noah's behaviour as immoral. We are given further insight into the character of Noah: when he is caught by Bumble he immediately blames Charlotte for his behaviour.

Chapter 28

Fleeing from the scene of the burglary, in order to ease his escape, Sikes drops the unconscious Oliver into a ditch and leaves him for dead. Hours later Oliver comes round: weak and delusional he makes his way to the nearest house. At length Oliver realises it is the same house that Sikes attempted to burgle the night before, but in desperation he knocks at the door. He is identified by the house servants as one of the 'thieves' and he is dragged into the house. He is so ill that a doctor is sent for.

Dishonour amongst thieves

Sikes is prepared to shoot Toby Crackit if he does not help him with the

Crime

wounded Oliver. Crackit is only concerned with self-preservation and advises Sikes to 'drop the kid and show 'em your heels.' Eventually, to protect himself, Sikes leaves Oliver behind. Why does he take Oliver out of the house? Is it because he feels some responsibility for the boy, or is it just to protect himself from exposure?

' "I'll tell you what it is, gentlemen," said he, "we're all afraid." '

The introduction of Brittles and Giles provides us with some much needed comedy as their brave pursuit of the robbers gradually stutters into fear and uncertainty. Note the difference in humour used by Dickens here. Dickens is much less scathing than he is with, say, the cowardice of Mr Bumble. It is a gentle humour which is more affectionate than satirical.

'He summoned up his strength for one last trial ...'

Oliver

Once more Oliver finds himself in a dangerous situation. The odds are stacked against him, yet Dickens again shows Oliver as a fighter and a survivor. Giles tells his story of disturbing the robbers with wonderful exaggeration and bravado. Notice the reaction of Giles when there is a knock at the door and he fears the criminals have returned. Rose Maylie shows nothing but sympathy and concern for the welfare of a suspected criminal. Does this affect the way we view Rose?

Chapter 29

We are introduced to the Maylie household. The doctor arrives and the patient is visited.

An earthly angel

There is no doubt that Dickens wishes us to view Rose in a particular way. Look at the language he uses to describe her, 'angel', 'mild and gentle', 'pure and beautiful'. She is almost too good for this earth! Compare the presentation of Rose with that of Fagin in Chapter 8. Are the two characters described in a believable way? If not, why do you think Dickens includes characters like this?

'more from good-humour than from good living ...'

The arrival of the doctor introduces another pleasant, eccentric character. The doctor's good nature is to prove crucial for Oliver in subsequent chapters.

Chapter 30

The Maylies and the doctor are surprised to find that the thief is only a small child and an innocent-looking one at that. Sensing his innocence, they hatch a plan to save Oliver from the constable.

Poverty

The doctor suggests that, though it is surprising, even the young and innocent-looking can be drawn into crime. Rose Maylie speaks eloquently about the possible causes, one of which is 'want of bread', and convinces Mrs Maylie to have mercy on Oliver. Rose's compassion is heightened by the fact that she has been an orphan too and she feels a strong bond with Oliver.

Chapter 31

The Bow Street Officers arrive. The doctor and the Maylies are concerned about Oliver and the danger of his being arrested. Mr Losberne makes up a story about Oliver being 'accidentally wounded by a spring-gun in some boyish trespass' and suggests he has been wrongly accused by Giles. Giles, fearing that he has done the boy an injustice, cannot swear that Oliver is the housebreaking boy. Oliver is cleared of any involvement in the crime and is taken into the care of the Maylies.

The arrival of the Bow Street Officers

Crime

Blathers and Duff are presented as buffoons. They are fairly ineffective as detectives and spend most of their time at the Maylies telling the absurdly humorous story of Conkey Chickweed who staged his own robbery. It is significant that they are easily fooled by the doctor's story. Are there any other examples of the law being represented in an ineffective way?

Chapter 32

Oliver recovers at the Maylie house and he is grateful for their kindness. Mr Losberne takes Oliver to visit Mr Brownlow, only to find that the kind old gentleman has left for the West Indies. The pair return to Chertsey and then the family moves to a cottage in the country. Here Oliver spends three months during which he is educated and cared for.

The incident at Chertsey Bridge

As Oliver and the doctor are travelling to visit Mr Brownlow Oliver mistakenly identifies the house he believes to be the hideout of Sikes and Toby Crackit, where they had spent the night before the attempted burglary of the Maylies'. The doctor, without thinking and in a rage, impetuously enters the house to bring the villains to justice. Of course Oliver is shown to be mistaken. Why do you think Dickens includes this scene? Is he saying something about the character of Losberne? Or does it show the total belief the doctor has in Oliver?

The country versus the town

It is worth considering Dickens' presentation of the countryside in this chapter. He appears to romanticise the countryside and it, in some way, repairs Oliver both spiritually and physically. Dickens' description of the town is generally less favourable.

A period of happiness for Oliver

Oliver's stay at the Maylies' shows him developing further as a character. It is here that Oliver begins to learn to read and write and, because of the country air, becomes fitter and stronger.

Oliver

Chapter 33

Rose Maylie falls ill. She has a 'dangerous fever' which is life-threatening. Oliver is sent to the George Inn in the nearby town to deliver letters to be sent to Mr Losberne and Mrs Maylie's son, Harry. On his way out of the inn Oliver bumps into Monks who reacts in a bizarre way which disturbs Oliver. With more important things on his mind Oliver returns to the house to find that Rose's condition has worsened. Mr Losberne arrives and Rose falls into a deep sleep from which she will either awaken and recover or slip into death. Hours later the doctor, Mr Losberne, enters with the good news that Rose has woken and will, therefore, survive the illness.

Oliver comes face to face with Monks

By chance Oliver comes across the perpetrator of so much of his misery, but he is completely unaware of the fact. Consider Monks' reaction. He is

Chance

surprised and shocked at meeting Oliver and is also 'fearful'. He is described, then, almost as if he is a wild animal: he has a 'wild look' and he 'gnashes his teeth'. Why does Dickens describe him in this way? How do you view Monks at this point in the text?

Rose's illness

Just as Oliver seems to have found some lasting happiness fate deals another blow. Rose is suddenly taken ill and it soon becomes a matter of life and death. Some critics have seen the illness of Rose as an unnecessary distraction, further adding to Dickens' over-sentimental presentation of her character. Perhaps Dickens includes this episode to show that even the characters who have pleasant lives still have to face reality at times and endure suffering and pain.

■ Self-test questions Chapters 14–33

Who? What? Why? When? Where? How?

1   Who pretends to be Oliver's sister?
2   What is Mr Losberne's profession?
3   Why does Bill Sikes need Oliver for the burglary?
4   When does Mr Bumble see the advertisement concerning Oliver?
5   Where does Fagin look for Bill Sikes?
6   How much of a reward is offered for information about Oliver?
7   Who is Bill Sikes' partner in crime?
8   What reason does Mr Losberne give for Oliver's injury?
9   Why does Bill Sikes show Oliver his pistol?
10   When does Old Sally admit to stealing the locket belonging to Oliver's mother?
11   Where does Mr Brownlow send Oliver on his errand?
12   How old is Rose when she first appears in the novel?

Who said this about whom?

1   'He's an out-and-out Christian ...'
2   'We have just heard a full account of him from his birth; and he has been a thorough-paced little villain, all his life.'
3   'Heaven will never let her die so young.'
4   'stop, you white-livered hound.'
5   'I saw it was not easy to train him to the business ... he was not like other boys in the same circumstances.'

Open quotations

Complete the following quotations.

1   'I tell you again, it was badly planned. Why not have kept him ...'
2   ' "The child," said the girl, suddenly looking up, ...'
3   'The scanty parish dress, the livery of his misery ...
4   'As he glided stealthily along, creeping beneath the shelter of the walls and doorways, ...'

Prove it !
1   How far is Mr Bumble presented as being selfish and cruel in this section?
2   'Dickens often uses comedy to relieve tension.' Give examples to show how
     far you agree with this statement.

Chapter 34

Harry Maylie arrives with Giles to find that Rose is recovering from her illness. During a conversation with his mother it becomes clear that Harry wishes to marry Rose, but there is something mysterious in Rose's past that Mrs Maylie suggests may be frowned upon by society and eventually ruin their relationship. Harry and Oliver become firm friends. One evening Oliver drifts into sleep while reading at his desk and wakes to see the faces of Fagin and Monks staring in through the window. Before Oliver can raise the alarm they disappear.

Harry's love for Rose

Harry, it appears, is very much in love with his cousin Rose and wishes to marry her. Mrs Maylie suggests there is something dubious about Rose's background and advises against marrying 'a wife on whose name there is a stain, which, though it originate in no fault of hers ... may be visited upon her'. Rose's 'doubtful birth' links her again to Oliver.

Faces at the window

The chapter ends with Oliver being awoken from a sleep by two terrifying faces glaring in at him through his study window. It is almost as if the figures are a figment of Oliver's imagination, and the event is at once shocking and disturbing. The threat of Fagin and Monks invades Oliver's tranquil life and comes as a distinct reminder that Oliver's safety is still in jeopardy. The criminal element is never far from Oliver's life.

Chapter 35

The pursuit of Fagin and Monks is unsuccessful. Rose gradually recovers from her illness. Harry and Rose have a conversation in which Harry declares his love for her and his wish to marry her. Rose, to save Harry from any scandal, refuses even though it is obvious she loves him. Harry asks her to allow him to raise the matter once more in a year's time.

The mysterious disappearance

There is no trace whatsoever of the presence of Monks or Fagin. They seem to disappear into thin air. Why does Dickens do this? Are we meant to think it is all in Oliver's mind? Or is it in keeping with previous descriptions of Monks and Fagin? Is there an element of the supernatural here? What effect is created by Dickens?

'there is a stain upon my name ...'

Loneliness

Rose feels she cannot marry Harry as this may disgrace him in the eyes of polite society, preventing him from progressing in his career which may make him resent her. She is destined for a lonely life. She sees herself as 'an obstacle to (Harry's) progress in the world.' She sacrifices her own happiness. Does Rose show moral strength at this point? She speaks 'firmly' to Harry and she will not give way. Her sense of what is right is similar to Oliver's, as is her dubious birth. Can you find examples in the text of Oliver's moral strength? Look at chapters 6, 10 and 22.

Chapter 36

Harry leaves for London with Mr Losberne, but before he goes he strikes a deal with Oliver. He asks Oliver to write to him once a fortnight to the General Post Office in London concerning his mother and Rose. The request is given added weight by it being a 'secret' arrangement. Oliver is happy to agree. Harry leaves as Rose watches, tearfully, from an upstairs window.

Harry's trust in Oliver

Oliver

Oliver is definitely maturing and is entrusted with an adult responsibility by Harry. Oliver's character has developed significantly. Look back to how he is first viewed by the Maylie family in Chapter 30. How far has Oliver progressed in such a short space of time?

Chapter 37

Mr Bumble has been promoted to workhouse master and has married Mrs Corney. Married life is hardly what Mr Bumble had expected, as Mrs Bumble is bossy and domineering. In a crucial power struggle Mrs Bumble violently attacks Mr Bumble. Mr Bumble escapes in a daze, only to encounter his wife again in the laundry room where she humiliates him in front of the workhouse paupers. In disgrace Mr Bumble leaves the workhouse and seeks out a public house where he can drown his sorrows. By chance Mr Bumble meets Monks. Monks, ironically, has been looking for Mr Bumble as he requires some information from him concerning the death of Old Sally. Bumble sees a chance to profit and worm his way back into Mrs Bumble's good books, so he tells Monks that he knows the last person to sit with Old Sally before she died. A meeting is arranged for the following evening.

'the lowest depth of the most snubbed henpeckery ...'

The reality of married life to a woman such as Mrs Bumble is comically shown through Mr Bumble's fearful obedience to his wife. Even though Bumble has been promoted, with his beadle's uniform gone, so has all of his authority.

What is Dickens trying to say about the character of Mr Bumble at the beginning of this chapter? Note the 'shrill voice' of Mrs Bumble and how she dominates and bullies Mr Bumble. Indeed, when Bumble attempts to stand up for himself and wishes aloud that Mr Corney were still alive so that he would not be in this situation, Mrs Bumble tries to make him feel guilty and gain the upper hand by crying, 'But, tears were not the things to find their way to Mr Bumble's soul'. This failing, Mrs Bumble physically attacks Mr Bumble who shows his cowardice by running away. Look closely at the passage where Mrs Bumble degrades Mr Bumble in front of the workhouse paupers. Notice how Mr Bumble 'submits', while Mrs Bumble 'demands'. Can you find any other examples of language used by Dickens to show that the power is shifting from Mr Bumble to his wife?

A chance meeting with a mysterious stranger

Once again the narrative is driven on by chance. The public house Mr

Chance

Bumble chooses to go into just happens to have Monks as a customer, and Monks just happens to be looking for the former beadle! It is interesting to consider the ease with which Monks sees Mr Bumble for what he is and not as he tries to appear, saying to him 'You have the same eye to your own interest, that you always had, I doubt not.' Does Monks recognise a fellow villain in Bumble? Who is the greater villain in the novel? What effect does Dickens create by delaying the revelation of Monks' name until the end of the chapter? You should have already worked out the identity of the mysterious stranger before the end of the chapter. What clues are given to help you work out his identity?

Chapter 38

The next evening Mr and Mrs Bumble arrive at Monks' address in the most run-down and derelict part of town. Monks wishes to know what Old Sally said on her deathbed about Oliver's mother. After negotiating a fee of £25 Mrs Bumble tells her story and reveals that she has a locket that Old Sally stole from Oliver's mother after she died. Monks gets rid of the locket by throwing it into the river through a sinister trap-door in the floor, and with it goes any evidence of Oliver's identity. After the act has been committed the three swear themselves to secrecy.

Mrs Bumble in charge

It is significant that it is Mrs Bumble, not her husband, who negotiates with Monks over a price for disclosing the information she has. This confirms the fact that it is Mrs Bumble who has the power in the relationship and is another humbling experience for Mr Bumble.

Environment

The actions of Monks here make him as much of a villain as any other character in the novel. Is Monks' treachery brought about by the environment he inhabits, or is it in his nature?

The evidence is destroyed

Crime

The devilry of Monks is at its height in this chapter. He is a strange and twisted character. Look at the way he has a 'fit' after hearing the thunder, and his increasing excitement as Mrs Bumble reveals the story told to her by Old Sally. The dramatic way he disposes of the locket and ring, through a trap-door into the river, adds to the horrific feel of this chapter.

Chapter 39

Sikes is ill and confined to bed with a fever after his failed attempt at burglary. Nancy, who has been caring for Sikes, is also 'pale and reduced' and, after helping Sikes to a chair, faints. At this moment Fagin, the Dodger and Charley enter and revive her. This is the first time Fagin has contacted Sikes and Nancy for three weeks, although he calms Bill by saying that he has brought food and drink for them. Sikes asks Fagin for some money which Nancy is to fetch. Later, as Fagin is in the process of finding the money, Monks arrives. Fagin takes him up to a second-storey room so they can talk privately. Nancy sneaks up the stairs and listens to their conversation. Eventually Fagin returns and gives Nancy the money she has been waiting for and she returns to Sikes. Nancy is agitated and nervous; Sikes questions her manner and puts it down to fever before he finally falls asleep. It becomes apparent that Nancy has put laudanum (a sleeping drug) into Sikes' drink which has knocked him out. Nancy rushes out and hurries through the London streets to arrive at the residence of Mrs Maylie. She eventually succeeds in getting a message to Rose Maylie that she wishes to speak to her urgently.

An ungrateful patient

Even though Nancy has nursed Bill through his illness at considerable cost to

Sikes and Nancy

her own health he still treats her badly. Nancy's tenderness towards Bill is shown clearly at the start of the chapter. For a comparison look at Chapter 16. Why do you think Nancy loves Bill and why does Dickens go to such lengths to show that she will tolerate Bill's behaviour towards her? Does this make Nancy's betrayal more convincing and more heroic?

A touch of mystery and suspense

When Monks arrives at Fagin's den it is significant that Nancy recognises his voice. This indicates that it was her shadow that Monks saw in Chapter 26, and that she overheard his previous conversation with Sikes. Dickens creates suspense for the reader by not disclosing the full details of the conversation between Monks and Fagin. Does Dickens use this technique at any other point in the novel? Suspense is built up further by Nancy's reaction to the conversation which forces her towards 'some bold and hazardous step.'

The decision

Does Sikes have a presentiment of the future when he says, 'You're not a-going to – No, damme! you wouldn't do that!'? We are given further insight into their relationship, as even when Sikes is complimenting Nancy there is an element of threat in what he says. After Nancy has had to resort to putting laudanum in Sikes' drink to make him sleep, there is a moving moment as she 'kisses the robber's lips.'

Chapter 40

Nancy meets with Rose and she tells her everything she knows about Monks. She reveals that she overheard a conversation which linked Monks to the planned downfall of Oliver. She then describes how evidence of Oliver's identity is now at the bottom of the river and that, indeed, Monks is Oliver's brother and his motive has been to stop Oliver from claiming his rightful inheritance. Rose, recognising goodness in Nancy and her actions begs her to remain in safety and not to return to the dangerous underworld of crime she inhabits. For the love (and fear?) of Sikes Nancy says she must return. However, Nancy agrees to meet with Rose again, if she remains alive, by visiting London Bridge every Sunday night between 11 and 12 o'clock. Rose offers Nancy some money, but she proudly refuses then leaves.

Two different worlds

The contrast between Rose and Nancy is worth looking at in this chapter. Nancy feels ashamed of her lowly status while, true to form, Rose is considerate and understanding. Nancy clearly shows the link between poverty, environment and crime. Do you feel sympathy for Nancy at this point? Are her actions heroic? How great a risk is she taking?

Poverty

Environment

Note how Nancy feels that she is completely trapped in an environment of crime. Even when Rose Maylie offers her an escape route Nancy declines and says that the only way out for her is death.

42

Some answers are provided, some questions raised

Throughout this chapter we are given crucial pieces of information. By

Chance

chance Monks saw Oliver just before he was lost to Fagin's gang and taken in by Mr Brownlow. A deal was struck with Fagin to retrieve Oliver and lead him into a life of crime which would eventually ruin him. The next shock is that Monks is Oliver's brother and that he has destroyed evidence of Oliver's identity so that there is no danger of him losing

the 'young devil's money' now. Nancy also says that Rose and Oliver are connected to each other in some way. Dickens provides some answers here, but what questions does he raise? Why does Nancy go back? What irony is there in the statement Nancy makes about Bill, 'I am drawn back to him … and I should be, I believe, if I knew that I was to die by his hand at last.'?

Chapter 41

Rose is unsure whom to turn to with the information she has received from Nancy. At this moment Oliver bursts in with the news that he has seen Mr Brownlow. Without hesitation Rose and Oliver visit the kindly old gentleman. Rose relates Oliver's sorry history from the time that he disappeared from Mr Brownlow's care, and the two are reunited. When Oliver is busy with Mrs Bedwin, Rose also reveals Nancy's story to Mr Brownlow and asks for his help. Mr Brownlow speaks to Mr Losberne who, as Rose predicted, wants to rush in and quickly solve the problem. However, Mr Brownlow says patience is the key, that Monks must be 'brought to his knees' and to do this they must plan carefully. Mr Brownlow seeks the aid of Mr Grimwig, and Mr Losberne requests the help of Harry Maylie to execute the plan.

Chance to the rescue

Chance

Once again chance plays a key part in driving the plot of the novel forward. Just as Rose is despairing of whom to ask for help her prayers are answered by the sighting by Oliver of Mr Brownlow. Do you think Dickens' use of coincidence ever goes too far, or is it a necessary device used to tie the plot together?

'we must proceed gently and with great care.'

Mr Brownlow

Mr Brownlow is shown as more than just a kindly old gentleman in this chapter. He is determined to ensure that the people who have mistreated Oliver are brought to justice and he calmly takes control of the situation. It is evident that Mr Brownlow has a keen intelligence and the resources to ensure justice is done.

Chapter 42

Noah Claypole and Charlotte Sowerberry have stolen money from Mr Sowerberry's till and run away to London. They eventually end up at The Three Cripples. Fagin enters the public house and, hearing of strangers in town, spies on the couple. He decides, after listening to Noah's conversation and observing his behaviour, that he may be of some use to him. Fagin makes the couple's acquaintance, and as they talk he reveals that he knows the types of criminals Noah has been looking for and that he will help him find a buyer for his stolen money and provide him with a job.

A life of crime

Dickens provides us with dark humour with the reintroduction of Noah

Crime

Claypole. Indeed, the former charity boy (who now calls himself Morris Bolter) has the makings of an excellent criminal. What evidence can you find to prove this? What are your feelings about the relationship between Noah and Charlotte? Does it remind you of any other relationships in the novel? Why does Noah change his name? What does this say about his character?

Chapter 43

The freshly named Morris Bolter (Noah Claypole) meets again with Fagin. Fagin's hold over Noah is immediately established when Fagin reminds him that he knows of Noah's involvement in the Sowerberry robbery. Fagin is particularly keen to add new members to his gang as, we find out, the Dodger has been arrested for pick-pocketing and will more than likely be transported. Noah is sent by Fagin to find out what happens at the Dodger's trial. Noah arrives at the courthouse and sees the Dodger make for himself 'a glorious reputation' by showing a dramatic but humorous contempt for the court and the legal system. The Dodger is sentenced to transportation and is led away.

'it's your object to take care of number one ...'

We are given an insight into Fagin's philosophy of self-preservation. He is

Crime

concerned with protecting himself and looking after his own interests and no one else's. He immediately makes Morris (Noah) feel dependant on him. Look for key words that describe the growing relationship between Fagin and Noah Claypole, such as 'respect' and 'fear'. Fagin shows his power over Noah by forcing him to visit the courthouse for the artful

Dodger's trial. Noah's cowardice and fear of exposure show how easily he has fallen into Fagin's web of crime and control.

The trial of the artful Dodger

It is in this chapter we find out the Dodger has been arrested. Charley Bates, his partner in crime, is not upset about the fact that the Dodger has been

Crime

arrested, but is concerned that he has been arrested for such a petty crime. He feels that the Dodger will not be remembered for the expert criminal he is. We also see the Dodger's true worth to Fagin. He has stolen a cheap snuff box and Fagin generously says 'Ah! he was worth fifty boxes, and I'd give the price of as many to have him back.' Ultimately Fagin has used the Dodger as he would use anybody. At the trial the Dodger shows utter contempt for the legal system and plays to the public gallery like an actor. He pretends he has been done a great injustice and that he is a gentleman, to the delight of the crowd. He mocks the court and the jury, but his victory is a hollow one as he is still sentenced to transportation. What is your final view of the Dodger? Are you relieved that he does not suffer the same fate as Sikes and Fagin? If so, why is this, do you think?

Chapter 44

Nancy attempts to leave the company of Sikes and Fagin to keep her secret engagement with Rose Maylie. Sikes violently refuses to allow Nancy to 'take a breath of air'. Nancy is desperate to leave but is forcibly held back by Sikes. Fagin leaves the house considering plans of how to use Nancy, who he believes has a new lover, to bring about the death of the dangerous villain Sikes.

Nancy is not seen as an innocent; she even feels close and connected to Fagin. She makes sacrifices for Sikes who attempts to control her. Compare the relationship of Sikes and Nancy with that of Noah Claypole and Charlotte at the beginning of Chapter 42. Are there any similarities? How are women generally presented in the novel?

A glimpse of the devil?

Fagin

Fagin's hand is described as a 'withered old claw' and he is called a 'devil' by Sikes. Fagin shows his true colours again as he suggests to Nancy that they should get rid of Sikes. Fagin sees the opportunity to 'poison' Sikes. He sees the death of Sikes as strengthening his own position.

Chapter 45

Fagin employs Bolter (Noah) on a secret mission to follow and spy on Nancy. The following Sunday Fagin leads Noah to The Three Cripples and points out Nancy to him. As she leaves the public house Noah follows her.

The cowardice of Noah is comical. He refers to himself proudly as a 'cunning sneak'. It is interesting to note that even Fagin cannot guess at the real reason for Nancy's nervousness and agitation. He, like Sikes, believes at this point that Nancy would never betray her own kind. What are Nancy's reasons for risking her own life?

Chapter 46

Nancy, followed expertly by 'Bolter', meets with Mr Brownlow and Rose Maylie. They talk on the steps of the bridge, and the conversation is overheard by 'Bolter'. During this exchange Nancy gives a description of Monks and Mr Brownlow recognises the description. Mr Brownlow offers Nancy the chance of escaping to safety, but she refuses. They part company and Noah Claypole (Bolter) rushes back to Fagin's house to relate what he has heard.

The tragic figure of Nancy

Sikes and Nancy

Nancy is petrified; she almost senses that she will soon die. Mr Brownlow has faith in Nancy. Mr Brownlow wants her to agree to betray Fagin if Monks will not confess. However, because of Nancy's strong loyalty she refuses to do this. Even when Mr Brownlow offers her a chance to escape from her desperate life she feels she cannot accept.

Chapter 47

Noah Claypole reports back to Fagin about Nancy's meeting. Fagin immediately meets with Bill Sikes. Fagin asks Bill what he would do if anyone betrayed them. Sikes' response is suitably violent. Noah Claypole repeats his story to Bill who, in a fury, returns home to Nancy and, in spite of her appeals for mercy, brutally murders her.

A black heart

Look at the description of Fagin towards the beginning of the chapter. Dickens

Fagin

again describes him as being less like a human and more like a hideous phantom. Fagin skilfully manipulates Sikes by building up to revealing Nancy's betrayal by asking him what he would do if anyone did such a thing. There is an understanding between Sikes and Fagin that Nancy will be killed. It is a heart-stopping moment in the text.

The death of Nancy

This incident is brutal and hard-hitting. Nancy begs for her life, proclaiming that she has not betrayed Bill. The cruelty of Sikes is horrific. In spite of his rage he can still think clearly enough not to fire the gun because the noise it would

make might raise the alarm, so instead beats her in the face and head with it. Sikes almost cannot look at Nancy as she holds the handkerchief up to heaven, but he then finishes the job by beating her to death with a club. This is a scene of graphic violence and, at the time in which it was written, would have been extremely shocking to the reader, as it still is today.

Examiner's tip

While this passage is extremely violent, it is arguably the most gripping in the whole novel. Sikes' actions are horrific, yet the chapter makes compulsive reading. The detailed description of Sikes' repulsive crime gives us an insight into the violent world of crime in nineteenth-century London and into the mind of a brutal killer. See the question on page 57.

Chapter 48

In the morning Sikes leaves the room where he has committed the murder and travels towards the country. He doesn't know where to go and he ends up in a public house, but decides to leave when he overhears a conversation between two men who are discussing Nancy's murder, news of which has now spread. He decides to return to London. Realising he may be identified by his dog, he decides to drown it, but the dog senses what he intends to do and runs away: Sikes continues his journey alone.

The conscience of a murderer

There is a ghoulish opening to the chapter as Sikes attempts to cover the body

of Nancy with a rug and then removes it. Nancy has been reduced to a lump of blood and flesh. Blood, indeed, is everywhere, splattered on the murderer himself and even on the feet of the dog. It is a gruesome scene and Dickens expertly describes Sikes' state of mind. Fear and guilt begin to consume Sikes and he hurriedly leaves the scene of the crime. His fear of capture is almost as bad as his fear of his brutal actions: Nancy seems to be haunting him already.

Chapter 49

Monks is captured and brought to Mr Brownlow's residence. Mr Brownlow threatens him with the full weight of the law if he doesn't talk. Reluctantly Monks agrees. We find out that Mr Brownlow does indeed know Monks and was, in fact, his father's best friend. Monks' real name is Edward Leeford and Mr Brownlow was to have married his father's sister, but she tragically died. Monks' father had married, but it was an arranged marriage that turned out to be a bad match. The couple ended up hating each other so they separated. Monks' father, Edwin Leeford, stayed at home and became friends with a retired naval officer and his two daughters. The elder of the two girls fell in love with Monks' father and they began a relationship. Monks' father was called away to Rome where he had inherited money from a relative. Before he left the country he saw Mr Brownlow and left with him a portrait of the girl he had fallen in love with. He was desperate and wanted to sell all his property to make some money. While in Rome he took ill himself and died without apparently leaving a will, therefore, all the money went directly to his wife. After this Mr Brownlow had tried to find the naval officer's family, but they had left their home and could not be traced. It eventually comes to light that the young girl has become pregnant and has left her family for fear of disgrace. Edwin Leeford is obviously the father.

Mr Brownlow then tells of finding Oliver and realising that he bore a remarkable resemblance to the portrait. When Oliver went missing Mr Brownlow knew that Monks would be the only person to solve the mystery of Oliver's identity. Mr Brownlow left for the West Indies where Monks was supposedly living.

Monks denies any knowledge of Oliver's existence, but Mr Brownlow insists that he does and repeats the conversation Monks had with Fagin concerning the locket. Brownlow suggests that Nancy has been murdered as a direct result of Monks' actions. At this point Monks breaks down and says he will confess. Brownlow also tells Monks that he has to give Oliver his rightful inheritance.

Mr Losberne enters and reveals that there is a reward on Bill Sikes' head and, as his dog has been sighted in London, he will probably be arrested imminently. Fagin's capture is also expected to follow.

The evil of Monks

Crime

We find out that the sole reason for Monks' obsession with destroying Oliver is to protect his fortune and ensure that his half-brother never inherits his rightful share. He would go to any lengths to achieve this end.

The determination of Mr Brownlow

Mr Brownlow

Once again Mr Brownlow shows that he is a determined character. He almost single-handedly forces Monks to confess and secures the financial future of Oliver through his actions.

Chapter 50

In a run-down part of London called Jacob's Island the exposed criminals Toby Crackit and Tom Chitling are hiding out. We learn that Fagin has been arrested and that Bet, who has gone mad when identifying Nancy's body, has been taken to hospital. Fagin, it is thought, will be sentenced to death as an accessory to murder. Sikes' dog then arrives at the hide-out and the criminals fear that his master may soon follow. Sure enough, Sikes soon knocks at the door and is allowed into the house. Charley Bates then arrives. He is horrified that Sikes is there and attacks him for what he has done to Nancy, but Sikes is too strong for him. However, Charley's cries alert the public and a large crowd gathers. Sikes tries to escape the mob by lowering himself with a rope from the house into a surrounding ditch. As he puts the rope over his head, to place under his armpits, Sikes sees a vision of Nancy's eyes, slips, and inadvertently hangs himself. Bulls-eye, the dog, tries to leap onto his master's shoulders, misses, and falls to his death too.

The redemption of Charley

Crime

Charley Bates turns against Sikes and helps the crowd to find where Sikes is hiding. He calls him a monster and says he will give him up. Contrast Charley here with elsewhere in the novel. Why is it so important that it is Charley who attacks Sikes?

A violent justice

Sikes and Nancy

The death of Sikes is gruesome and, in some ways, fitting for the brutal and violent criminal. It is interesting that it is Sikes' conscience that leads to his slipping on the rooftop and plunging to his death. What is your final opinion of Sikes? Are you satisfied that his life ends in this way?

Chapter 51

The Maylies, Mr Losberne, Mr Brownlow and Oliver return to Oliver's birthplace. Here Oliver is introduced to Monks. Oliver recognises him as the man he saw outside the George Inn and who looked through his window with Fagin. Monks admits that Oliver is his half-brother. He reveals that his father wrote a letter to Agnes, Oliver's mother, when he was ill and that he had also left a will. The will provided an annual income for Monks and his mother, but the bulk of the fortune was to be divided equally between Agnes Fleming and her son, Oliver. Monks' mother burned the will. The Flemings, fearing shame because of an illegitimate child, moved to another part of the country and changed their name. Agnes left the family home and the old man, after searching for her in vain, finally died of a broken heart. On his own mother's deathbed Monks swore to find the illegitimate child of Agnes Fleming and destroy him. Monks admits to buying the locket from the Bumbles and disposing of it. Mr and Mrs Bumble are brought in by Grimwig and the story of the locket is confirmed. For their part in the episode Mr Brownlow assures them they will never be 'employed in a situation of trust again.' Monks then identifies Rose Maylie as Agnes Fleming's orphaned sister, who has been brought up under a cloud of shame because Monks' mother had told the people who adopted Rose (and from whom Mrs Maylie had subsequently taken her) that the girl was illegitimate. Rose is, therefore, Oliver's aunt. Harry Maylie arrives and asks Rose to marry him. He has become a clergyman so that no social barriers can prevent Rose from marrying him. The chapter ends with the sad news that Oliver's childhood friend little Dick is dead.

The story unfolds

Apart from the information received in this chapter, the hypocrisy of Mr Bumble is noteworthy. After his wife leaves, Mr Bumble tries to blame their misconduct on her. Mr Brownlow shows no mercy and says that Bumble is equally, if not more to blame than his wife. Mr Bumble, who has represented the authorities for years, suddenly turns on the system and woefully spits out his famous line, 'the law is a ass – a idiot'.

Chapter 52

Fagin is sentenced to death. He is led in a daze to the condemned cell. Mr Brownlow and Oliver visit him and ask him for the papers that Monks has entrusted to him, which presumably confirm in writing Oliver's identity. Fagin tells Oliver their whereabouts, then tries to persuade Oliver to help him escape. Fagin has clearly lost his mind. The chapter ends with 'the cross-beam, the rope, and all the hideous apparatus of death.'

Childhood

Compare the character of Oliver at the end of the text with the character of Scout at the end of *To Kill a Mockingbird*. Have both characters matured by the end of their respective novels? Have they lost any of their innocence? It is interesting to consider and compare the terrible events both characters have experienced during the course of the novels. See the question on page 55.

Loneliness

Fagin's isolation at the end of the text is pitiful, and Dickens' description of the condemned man makes for some disturbing reading. Fagin is desperate and repulsive. Contrast Fagin's final appearance with his first in Chapter 8. What differences can you identify? Is Dickens' presentation of him convincing at the end?

Examiner's tip

Even when the villains of the text are defeated Dickens still produces some of his most powerful, engaging and memorable writing. Note how, in this chapter, Dickens presents us with a harrowing and haunting picture of a broken man. See the question on page 57.

Chapter 53

Rose and Harry are married. Oliver receives his inheritance and shares it with his disgraced brother, Monks, who squanders the money and eventually dies overseas in prison. Mr Brownlow adopts Oliver as his son. Noah Claypole receives a pardon for his part in bringing about the arrest of Fagin and becomes a police informer. Mr and Mrs Bumble end up in the workhouse as a result of losing their positions and livelihoods. Charley Bates turns away from a life of crime and works in the country. The novel ends with Oliver restored to his rightful place and finally happy.

And they all lived happily ever after?

The parish boy's progress is complete at the end of the novel, while other characters pay dearly for their crimes. Is the ending of the novel a satisfactory one? Are you pleased to see justice prevail, or do you feel any sympathy towards any of the criminal characters? Has there been any cost to Oliver's happiness?

■ Self-test questions Chapters 34–53

Who? What? Why? When? Where? How?
1. Who spies on Nancy when she meets Rose Maylie and Mr Brownlow?
2. What does Monks throw into the river?
3. Why is the Dodger transported?
4. When do Noah Claypole and Charlotte Sowerberry travel to London?
5. Where does Nancy meet Rose and Mr Brownlow?
6. How does Sikes murder Nancy?
7. Who is Monks in relation to Oliver?
8. What happens to Fagin and Monks after they have peered through Oliver's window?
9. Why does Mr Bumble blame his wife for all their wrongdoing?
10. When does Harry ask Oliver to write to him?
11. Where does Fagin spend the last night of his life?
12. How does Sikes kill himself?

Who said this about whom?
1. 'If he hesitates or moves a finger but as you bid him, drag him into the street, call for the aid of the police and impeach him as a felon in my name.'
2. 'Oh! God forgive this wretched man!'
3. 'Do not close your heart against all my efforts to help you...'
4. 'And if we meet again, anywhere, there's no call for us to know each other – you understand?'
5. 'a creature as fair and innocent of guile as one of God's own angels ...'

Open quotations
Complete the following quotations.
1. 'there is a stain upon my name ...'
2. '"Denial to me is vain," replied Mr Brownlow. ...'
3. 'Blanched face, sunken eyes, hollow cheeks ...'

4 'You're a great deal too fond of poking your nose ...'

5 'I am about to put my life ...'

Prove it !

1 In your opinion, is justice done at the end of the novel?

2 How is the description of Fagin's last night alive made powerful and haunting by Dickens?

3 Why does Nancy help Oliver?

How to write a coursework essay

Most of you are probably studying *Oliver Twist* as part of a Wide Reading coursework assignment for GCSE English/English Literature. If we look at the requirement of the NEAB examinations, we find that this assignment must involve comparison between a complete pre-twentieth-century prose text and at least one suitable twentieth-century text. It is also essential to make certain comments on the historical, social and cultural background of the texts. Charles Dickens' novels are particularly suitable in this respect: his presentation of nineteenth-century society highlights many social and political issues of the time. In the following pages we examine some possible subjects for Wide Reading assignments. Throughout the **Text commentary** the **Essays icon** draws attention to useful material for your assignment.

There are, of course, some general principles for these assignments.

Comparison is essential. No credit is given for telling the story of all or part of *Oliver Twist* and that of a twentieth-century story with a similar theme. It is essential that you show that, while Charles Dickens draws his characters in a certain way, uses satire to make social comments and presents society in a variety of ways, your twentieth-century author does it differently, or exactly the same, or in a partly similar way. Therefore, your choice of twentieth-century comparison is important. There must be specific grounds for comparison. This can, of course, mean that the twentieth-century story is opposite in effect to Dickens; using similar ideas differently is a good ground for comparison.

The *most important consideration* in writing the essay is that it must develop an argument or explain a point of view consistently throughout. Choosing a title matters: if you write an essay called 'Childhood in *Oliver Twist* and *To Kill a Mockingbird*', you are not directing yourself to a specific comparison. The comparison should be made *throughout* the essay, not necessarily in the same sentence, but at least in adjacent paragraphs. Careful advance planning is also helpful in organising your theme or argument: making notes on the material, putting these notes in order, and then producing a draft of the essay. You should make a decision on what each paragraph is about, as far as possible signalling that to the reader in the opening sentence, often called a topic sentence because it states the topic of the paragraph.

In terms of length of essay, do bear in mind that it is only one of several pieces of coursework and there is no need for a 5,000 word blockbuster. Many essays will exceed 1,000 words: by how much depends on the material you wish to present and the advice of your teacher.

Crime and environment

To what extent are characters driven to crime by their environment in both Oliver Twist *by Charles Dickens and* Lord of the Flies *by William Golding?*

Crime is an essential theme in both of these texts, but to make your essay more specific the focus on environment and how that changes behaviour is an interesting point for comparison. Golding's novel shows how, when stranded on the island, the boys descend into savagery and murder. Examples of how and when this takes place and how the boys' actions are determined by the desperate situation they find themselves in could be compared to the willing descent into crime of characters such as Noah Claypole.

A comparison could be made between characters in both novels that resist crime in spite of their circumstances. Are there any similarities between Ralph in *Lord of the Flies* and Oliver, for instance? Both characters show a certain amount of moral strength by resisting crime and attempting to do what is viewed as morally acceptable by the society they find themselves isolated from. Ralph's various attempts to resist and fight against Jack Merridew could be compared to Oliver's attempts to withstand a life of crime.

What reasons are given by both writers for the existence of crime, and how far could it be said to be solely determined by the environments that characters are trapped in? A character like Nancy is worth looking at here. Even though Nancy shows she has the capacity for goodness she feels as if she is trapped into a certain way of behaviour. Are there any characters in *Lord of the Flies* who feel similarly trapped?

You may wish to argue that some characters in both texts are more prone to 'evil' than others and that, while their environment is a factor in determining their behaviour, sometimes their actions are difficult to explain and seem to be related to other factors as well, such as greed and power. The obvious comparision here is between characters such as Jack Merridew in *Lord of the Flies* and Monks in *Oliver Twist*.

Social issues and poverty

Oliver Twist *is a novel concerned with the hardships faced by a young Victorian orphan. What similarities, if any, exist between the central character in Dickens' novel and that of Billy Casper in* A Kestrel for a Knave *by Barry Hines?*

The scope for comparison of these two central characters is enormous. Both characters are isolated, bullied and neglected. Both characters are drawn by poverty into crime. Would you consider both characters to be victims ? What are the most obvious differences between the two? For example, is Billy always innocent in *A Kestrel for a Knave*, and to what extent does he cause the problems he experiences? Contrast this with Oliver, who very rarely acts inappropriately in the novel by Dickens. Both characters come from deprived backgrounds and yet behave very differently.

You could compare Oliver's treatment at the workhouse with Billy's home life and describe in detail their experiences and whether there are any similarities or differences. The social standing of both characters is important too. Billy and Oliver are used and abused by other characters in the text. Compare the treatment of Oliver by Mr Bumble and/or Sikes and the way Billy is bullied by Sugden and Jud. How do both characters cope with this mistreatment? Do any characters show the children in these texts kindness? Think about comparing Mr Farthing with Mr Brownlow for example. What are their motives for the way they treat each of the boys in their respective novels?

The historical contexts of both novels could be explored, too. How far is society different? Are attitudes the same? What kind of education does Oliver receive and how is it different from Billy's? At the end of the novels whose future is more promising and why is this? Do you feel both characters get what they deserve or are you dissatisfied with the outcome of either text?

Childhood

Both To Kill A Mockingbird *and* Oliver Twist *are concerned with children who grow up and mature through the course of the texts. Which presentation of childhood, in your opinion, is more convincing and why?*

You will have to do some research concerning the historical context of both these novels if you are to answer this essay question effectively. Even though *Oliver Twist* is set in Victorian England and *To Kill a Mockingbird* in the deep south of 1930s America there are some points of contact. Both Scout and Oliver view the world through innocent eyes and encounter prejudice and hatred that they do not really understand.

There are obvious differences, too, which you could discuss at length. Scout appears to be a much more active character than Oliver and actually challenges the prejudice she encounters, even if it is unwittingly, in Chapter 15 of *To Kill a Mockingbird*. Oliver, for the most part, is fairly passive, although he does show signs of spirit, particularly in Chapter 6. While Oliver appears to be morally intact at the end of the novel, Scout appears to have undergone experiences which change her outlook (the unfair trial of Tom Robinson, the realisation that Boo Radley is not a monster etc). Oliver does mature, but essentially clings to his moral values: Scout matures through childhood to view the world differently and broadens her moral outlook.

The narrative styles of both texts are different and you might comment on how this affects the way in which you view each of the characters. The narrator in *To Kill a Mockingbird* is Scout looking back and commenting on her childhood, while *Oliver Twist* is a third person narrative in which the author comments on the progress of the characters through the text.

What is gained through writing a first person narrative in *To Kill a Mockingbird*? Does reading events through the innocent eyes of Scout enable the reader to understand her behaviour and circumstances more effectively than the third person view given in *Oliver Twist*? On the other hand, by using a third person narrative style, is Dickens able to give us a more objective and accurate view of Oliver? In other words, which narrative style is more effective and why? Provide examples to support your argument.

Overall both texts deal with the difficulties of growing up and comparisons and contrasts are easy to find.

■ How to write an examination essay

Though most of you will be required to write on *Oliver Twist* as part of your coursework, some of you may need to answer an examination question on it. This section considers one specific title on the novel, but also gives general advice on how to approach an English Literature examination essay.

It has been said that the most interesting and memorable characters in Oliver Twist *are the villains. How far would you agree with this statement?*

Before you start writing

- The first essential is thorough revision. It is important that you realise that even Open Book examinations require close textual knowledge. You will have time to look up quotations and references, but *only if you know where to look.*

- Read the questions very carefully, both to choose the best one and to take note of exactly what you are asked to do.

- Do not answer the question you *imagine or hope* has been set. In the case of the above question you will need to write in detail about various characters you consider to be villains and comment on the way Dickens presents them. As well as this you must compare these characters to others in the text so that you can make a judgement which either agrees or disagrees with the statement.

- Identify all the key words in the question that mention characters, events and themes, and instructions as to what to do, e.g. compare, contrast, comment, give an account, etc. In this case you are making value judgements about a specific set of characters and considering how they have been presented, and whether or not you *agree* with the statement in the question.

- Look at the points you have identified and jot down what you are going to say about each. You are being asked to comment on characters and how they are presented, not to re-tell the story of *Oliver Twist*.

- Decide in what order you are going to deal with the main points. Try and follow a logical argument in which you present a convincing case. This is an open question, so whatever your opinion is make sure you justify it with reference to the text.

Writing the essay

- The first sentences are important. Try to summarise your response to the question so the examiner has some idea of how you plan to approach it. For example: 'There is no doubt that the villains in *Oliver Twist* dominate the text. Dickens presents them in a way which entertains, shocks and horrifies his readers'. Jump straight into the essay; do not ramble on for a page and a half trying to explain your viewpoint. A personal response is rewarded, but you must always answer the question and constantly *refer back* to the title.

- Make sure you answer all of the question. Many students spend all their time answering just one part of a question and ignoring the rest. This prevents you gaining marks for the parts left out. For example, if you just wrote about the presentation of Fagin your answer would be limited. In the same way, failing to answer enough questions on the examination is a waste of marks which can always be gained most easily at the start of an answer.

- There is no 'correct' length for an essay. What you must do is spend the full time usefully in answering all parts of the question: spending longer than the allocated time is dangerous. It is an advantage if you can organise your time well enough to reach an elegant conclusion, but it is better to leave an essay without a conclusion than to fail to start the next question.

- Take care with presentation, spelling and punctuation. Generally you will be awarded marks for accurate writing. Try and ensure that your writing is legible too – the examiner must be able to read your handwriting if they are to award you marks! It is generally unwise to use slang or contractions (e.g. 'they've' for 'they have').

- Use quotation or paraphrase when it is relevant and contributes to the quality and clarity of your answer. In this case, much can be shown by discussing the way characters are described and how their actions affect the plot. Quotations could be used to show the way Dickens uses specific language to create a desired effect. For example, our fear and mistrust of Monks as a character is heightened by the way he moves about the text like a 'shadow'. The use of quotation is effective when it is used to back up a point you are making. Nearly always extended quotations are unhelpful and a waste of time.

■ Self test answers Chapters 1–13

The numbers in brackets show the chapter in which the answers can be found.

Who? What? Why? When? Where? How?
1 The artful Dodger (Jack Dawkins). (8)
2 He is a chimney sweep. (3)
3 To try and find out information about Oliver. (13)
4 After the fight with Noah Claypole and Oliver's subsequent punishment. (7)
5 In a street near Pentonville. (12)
6 Twenty miles. (8)
7 Mr Bumble. (2)
8 Plummy and Sham. (8)
9 Because he makes fun of Oliver's dead mother. (6)
10 After drawing lots in the workhouse when the boys are half starved. (2)
11 In the workhouse garden. (7)
12 Five pounds. (4)

Who said this about whom ?
1 Mr Fang to Mr Brownlow about Oliver. (11)
2 Mrs Mann about Mr Bumble. (2)
3 The gentleman in the white waistcoat about Oliver. (2)
4 Mrs Bedwin about Oliver. (12)
5 The magistrate to Mr Gamfield. (3)

Open quotations
1 'Dead men never repent; dead men never bring awkward stories to light.' (9)
2 ' "Please, sir," replied Oliver, "I want some more." ' (2)
3 'If he means to blab us among his new friends, we may stop his mouth yet.' (13)
4 'You're an insolent, impertinent fellow. How dare you bully a magistrate!' (11)

Prove it !
1 Dickens presents us with a very negative view of the workhouses. Examples of the terrible conditions and mistreatment are in abundance from Chapters 1 to 3.
2 Look closely at Chapter 10. Oliver is shocked and dismayed at the Dodger's attempt to steal. His reaction shows that he will never turn to crime.
3 The legal system, represented by Mr Fang in this section, is shown to be inefficient and overtly harsh. Mr Fang can only be viewed as an absurd character. He is unreasonable and aggressive and even turns on the innocent Mr Brownlow.

■ Self-test answers Chapters 14–33

The numbers in brackets show the chapter in which the answers can be found.

Who? What? Why? When? Where? How?
1 Nancy. (15)
2 A doctor. (29)
3 They need someone small enough to fit through the lattice window. (19)

4   When he is in London at a coaching inn. (17)
5   Initially he looks for Bill at the Three Cripples then at Bill's residence. (26)
6   The reward is five guineas. (17)
7   Toby Crackit. (19)
8   He says Oliver has been injured by a spring-gun whilst inadvertently trespassing. (31)
9   To scare Oliver into doing exactly as he is told. If he does not Sikes will shoot him. (20)
10   On her deathbed. (24)
11   To the bookseller's. (14)
12   16 ('She was not past seventeen'). (29)

Who said this about whom ?
1   Charley Bates about Bull's-eye (Sikes' dog). (18)
2   Mr Grimwig about Oliver. (17)
3   Oliver about Rose Maylie. (33)
4   Sikes to Toby Crackit. (28)
5   Fagin about Oliver. (26)

Open quotations
1   'I tell you again, it was badly planned. Why not have kept him here among the rest, and made a sneaking, snivelling pickpocket of him at once ?' (26)
2   ' "The child," said the girl, suddenly looking up, "is better where he is than among us ..." ' (26)
3   'The scanty parish dress, the livery of his misery, hung loosely on his feeble body ...' (17)
4   'As he glided stealthily along, creeping beneath the shelter of the walls and doorways, the hideous old man seemed like some loathsome reptile ...' (19)

Prove it !
1   Chapter 17 proves Mr Bumble's cruelty, particularly with regard to his treatment of Little Dick. Also, in this chapter, Mr Bumble effectively lies about Oliver so that he can claim Mr Brownlow's reward. Chapters 23 and 27 are filled with Bumble's selfishness and greed as he decides to marry Mrs Corney because of her possessions!
2   Dickens does use comedy to relieve tension. At crucial moments in the story he often switches the narrative. The comic scenes involving Mr Bumble and Mrs Corney split up the burglary scenes, for example. Dickens also presents us with other comic characters, such as Giles and Brittles, to contrast with the severity of the situation Oliver finds himself in.

■ Self-test answers Chapters 34–53

The numbers in brackets show the chapter in which the answers can be found.

Who? What? Why? When? Where? How?
1   Noah Claypole (Morris Bolter). (46)
2   A small gold locket containing two locks of hair and a plain gold wedding ring. (38)
3   For attempting to pick a pocket. (43)
4   After they have stolen money from Mr Sowerberry's till. (42)
5   On London Bridge. (46)

6   He beats her to death with his gun and a heavy club. (47)
7   Monks is Oliver's half-brother. (49)
8   They seem to disappear into thin air. (35)
9   He wants to keep his job as workhouse master. (51)
10   Just before he leaves for London. (36)
11   In one of the condemned cells. (52)
12   As he tries to escape he inadvertently hangs himself. (50)

Who said this about whom ?
1   Mr Brownlow about Monks. (49)
2   Oliver about Fagin. (52)
3   Rose Maylie to Nancy. (40)
4   Monks to Mr and Mrs Bumble. (38)
5   Harry Maylie about Rose. (35)

Open quotations
1   'there is a stain upon my name, which the world visits on innocent heads.' (35)
2   ' "Denial to me is in vain," replied Mr Brownlow. "I shall show you that I know more than that." ' (49)
3   'Blanched face, sunken eyes, hollow cheeks, beard of three days' growth, wasted flesh, short thick breath; it was the very ghost of Sikes.' (50)
4   'You're a great deal too fond of poking your nose into things that don't concern you, making everybody in the house laugh ...' (37)
5   'I am about to put my life, and the lives of others in your hands.' (40)

Prove it !
1   There does appear to be an underlying morality to the text as the villains do end up paying for their crimes. Look at the fates of Sikes, Monks and Fagin, for example. The 'good' characters, while they do suffer, are for the most part unscathed at the end of the novel. Of all the characters it is Nancy who arguably retains most sympathy at the end.
2   Look at the language used by Dickens in this section. He builds up suspense, firstly through the sentencing of Fagin, then further in the presentation of a desperate old man who is scared and reluctant to die. Fagin appears to lose much of his power and degenerates, particularly in the final scene with Oliver, into madness. The final line of Chapter 52 is, indeed, a haunting one.
3   There are some interesting reasons for Nancy helping Oliver. It appears she recognises something of herself in the young orphan and he seems to reawaken a natural humanity and compassion in her character. Her final sacrifice for Oliver is an heroic one.